Elizur Wright, Ellen M. Wright

Elizur Wright's Appeals for the Middlesex Fells and the Forests

Elizur Wright, Ellen M. Wright

Elizur Wright's Appeals for the Middlesex Fells and the Forests

ISBN/EAN: 9783337119508

Printed in Europe, USA, Canada, Australia, Japan

Cover: Foto ©ninafisch / pixelio.de

More available books at **www.hansebooks.com**

ELIZUR WRIGHT'S APPEALS

FOR THE

MIDDLESEX FELLS AND THE FORESTS

WITH A

SKETCH OF WHAT HE DID FOR BOTH

BY HIS DAUGHTER, ELLEN WRIGHT

"*The wit of the dead belongs to all the living.*"

PUBLISHED BY
THE MEDFORD PUBLIC DOMAIN CLUB
1893
REPUBLISHED BY ELLEN WRIGHT, 1904

PREFACE.

These Appeals were published in 1893 with the hope to aid the passage of the law by which the Metropolitan Park System was secured; and at that time, having a fuller faith than later developments now warrant, that Mr. Wright's purposes—though not his plan—had the approval of the Metropolitan projectors, and would therefore be regarded in the park management, I wrote a brief and, as facts later gained show, incomplete account of his own effort in behalf of the Fells and Forest, laying, as I thought would be most helpful, what emphasis I might upon such help as he received. In this same hope I obtained for the law in Medford a petition of some thousand names,—all masculine, and embracing all but *one* of the men considered politically influential or of high social standing. The law having passed, in accordance with our father's will—not written will, but the one he lived, and to which these Appeals are the witnesses—my brother and I donated to the new enterprise our share in Pine Hill and its surrounding woods, in acreage representing, at its earlier assessed value, the $5,000 which he had pledged to the success of his own plan, so that by this gift, and a salvation made on the sales of our family over those of other Fells owners similarly located, the later movement stands debtor to Mr. Wright's effort—not only for the infinitely larger fact that without it the Metropolitan Park idea would never have been conceived, much less brought to any degree of success—financially to the extent, on actual estimate, of $72,069. For reasons which I shall, as I proceed, let speak for themselves, they are now republished with the hope that their testimony to the necessity of tree and forest preservation generally, as well as to a less destructive treatment of the trees in his own Fells, especially the latter *under the present caterpillar infliction* which would seem to be destroying them fast enough, may still be heard. The motto of the park management in this destruction would seem too largely, *spare the worm and spoil the tree*, and its motive, if you will take note of such circumstantial "straws" in my historical matter as "show the direction" of the diplomatic "wind," too political. And they are also republished that I may have their aid in defending their author's memory against assertions which a careful reading of them ought to have told his defamer were false, and to this end I have substantially substituted for my original account one written later by invitation of the Somerville Historical Society.

INTRODUCTION.

"Blow, blow, thou wintry wind, thou art not so rude as man's ingratitude."

"Of all sad words of tongue or pen,
The saddest are these, it might have been."

Until some courageous man with his little band of followers, ready to wear the thorns and let others take the laurels, has gone ahead to pave the way, that hope-inspiring and oft quoted couplet—

"And ever the right comes uppermost
And ever is justice done"—

is in administrative affairs the reverse of true. Such is the greed of gain, the need of a living, and so all-pervading the Mammon rule that through whatever educational channel the rising effort is made it is met and, if possible, suppressed by an ever alert censorship, or, if it has power and persistence, by persecution; and in its service is not wanting that craven spirit which, masked under discipleship to his cause, for a price betrayed the reformer of Nazareth. Beranger has it personified in his "Mr. Judas"; and, in making public appeal against the destruction of the park's trees on the caterpillar-exterminating pretext, we did not ourselves fail to meet it. Of his Mr. Judas as spy over the press, the poet's verse runs:—

"This moral looker-on who pries,
And gossips far and wide,
Hints he's a journalist at times
And takes the liberal side,
But should we at our purpose hint
To claim the right all things to print,
Hush! hush! I'll whisper in your ear
I've just seen Judas hovering near."

It is of course the wealthy few and their prime ministers who compose the censorship, for it is the wealthy few unofficially, as well as officially, who hold the administrative rein; and to their self-enriching schemes alone is success easy. Republicanism is the outgrowth only where the wealth distribution—and per consequence administrative power—is equal, or at least fair; and largely responsible for the inequality under a government which by a division of its executive force *officially* is, in form, republican, lies the fact that not honesty, but *diplomacy* has ever been the National policy. My definition of diplomacy is taken from history, not the dictionary, and is derived from its own corrupt practices; for nothing in history has stronger proof than that power, unrestricted or practically so, inevitably leads to its own abuse; and through *diplomacy* in this republic the *chance* of anything like an equal prosperity has steadily diminished. The public money has been gained by an indirect tax or tariff drawing proportionately far more heavily upon the earnings of industry than the profits of capital, and, where it has been *formerly* direct, the inequality of chance has not been lessened, for the processes of gaining it have still been indirect. Assessments have been practically arbitrary, and, under plausible pretexts and false appraisals, based not on the present market value of the property or commodity taxed, but upon the financial demands of those self-enriching schemes, the latest of which has not only entailed upon the masses a money tax bidding fair to increase with coming generations, but has had its far more disastrous and criminal cost in blood and misery abroad, and—begging pardon of the brutes—in an enbruting demoralization at home, which has not stopped either at the death agony of that murder in the highest degree, war with intent to rob, but has gone on to its inevitable consequences, torture the most diabolical. As property directly taxed is extensively real estate, that safety and happiness insuring condition to a country, the possession of homes, is discouraged, and the many forced under the burden of rents,—of course, sufficiently high to more than cover, as does the tariff the tax of the trade monopolist, that of the land monopolist. And thus it is that selfishness and dishonesty have thriven, till trusts, another instrument of extortion and indirect tax, have been added to tariffs; trusts by which the poor are made to support the rich, and the "beggars in rags and tags" go hungry to feast the "one in a velvet gown," the King Midas with "asses' ears" under whose craze for gold and crazy "goldentouch" neither bread nor blood, work of God nor need of man, are spared, so that now it is greed of gain plays master, and fear of loss slave to its behests, while morally there has become established a silence far too near stagnation not in itself to breed into the corruption, and badly to need the stirring up which belongs to the cleansing processes of reform.

Mr. De Las Casas, chairman of the Park Commission, in a diplomatic sketch of the park movement published by the historical *New England Magazine*, August, 1898, attributes what he would have his readers consider Mr. Wright's failure to his lacking in practical sense; and with that sort of practical sense which, in order to gain for its object a precarious and too often short-lived success by yielding "right," "justice," truth, or any part of that object's practical worth to diplomatic expediency, tends to the increase of this corruption, he certainly had no fellowship. He was too far-seeing a reformer and too good a mathematician not to know the danger to civilization when, in any of her problems, the Mammon factor is allowed to cancel or greatly to diminish the moral, and too much of a man to favor wrong in furthering right. Whatever his enterprise or his measures for it, to so strengthen the moral factor as to diminish the Mammon,—not cancel it, for, though a born usurper, under moral direction it has its office,—and with it the necessity of such yielding, was no small part of his aim; and in his Fells effort he was especially successful. And it is also true that his reform programme had little in common with that of the so-called practical politician. Not his the gilded and guilty pen of indirection and falsehood, the course which promises fair and plays false,—

> "But a fine sense of right,
> And truth's directness,
> Meeting each·occasion
> Straight as a line of light."

Not his the crafty devices by which a selfish purpose is concealed or made to appear a generous one, or the practice of antagonizing nothing except the dead and helpless. To the upper dogs in the Mammon fight—watch-dogs over the public funds—as a price of favor he threw no conciliatory bones in the way of compromises. The danger to the success thus bought, of their teeth, later he had too often seen proved; and he knew that an honest bone of contention thrown with sufficient mental force would be quite as effective and the success, if achieved, of a more solid and lasting character. And least of all, in bringing his Fells cause to success, would he have made bones of its woods,—the flesh and blood covering of its rocky skeleton, the soul and secret of its Nature-designed beauty as well as the heart and lungs of its fullest beneficence to man. But so largely, under Metropolitan management, has this programme and this woods sacrifice—everywhere in the Fells and especially pronounced on Mr. Wright's former grounds—been the order as to justify the conclusion that his hopes have from the start been made the price of a favor and a purpose in which this fullest beneficence, in so far as possible and have a park at all, has little or no place. In the Fells and Blue Hills the city,—or mother of cities,—the metropolis, found the park features of her less fortune-favored population's greatest need,—the air purification of a forestal density and contiguity which, if protected from its enemies, natural and artificial, would in time and by wind agency make itself felt even in crowded homes the most remote; and a rambling ground the beauty and benefits of which to be accessible needed only paths and driveways, that dead wood should be removed, and the fields kept mowed so that therein the trees, singly, in groups or groves, should have a free chance to spread their branches and show how magnificent and majestic they can be. With these broader and more benevolent benefits at heart, Mr. Wright's effort not only aimed to secure the entire acreage within the natural Fells boundary, but that they might be extended beyond the limits of the metropolis his forest law of 1882 provided for the establishment of similar forest parks anywhere in Massachusetts. Nor was this interdependence of a carbon-exhaling metropolis with an oxygen-exhaling forest park without well-supported scientific indorsement. Under Mr. Wright's enlightenment it had also the public favor, and it was no more than his long and patient pioneer work had earned that at least in the Fells, the foster child of that work, if not in the Blue Hills, the Metropolitan consummators of his cause's success should have given this forest park a place. It would have been a magnificent scenic variety to the other parks of the System; and its Nature-given right and title to such place has the incidental, though unintentional support of their landscape architect's investigating report;* for, after describing and illustrating the Fells and Blue Hills as they are and might be, it says, "The extreme rockiness and poverty of the soil of most of the new domain make this pre-eminently 'park-like' type of landscape impracticable as well as inappropriate." But such justice to Mr. Wright's effort, to Nature's design, and a city's need they were far from yielding. Instead of the "pre-eminently 'park-like' type" so exquisitely illustrated in Forest Hills, Mt. Auburn, and other cemeteries, we are asked, or made to do it without the asking, to let our Fells Forest Park bird in the hand go for one in the bush of empirical value; and, in defence of a

* See " Vegetation and Scenery in the Metropolitan Reservations of Boston," by Charles Eliot. In quoting from this report, I shall omit reference to pages, as the reading matter is brief, and to fully support my statements the whole should be read.

large and profitable woods sacrifice in behalf of this substitute for scenery in which the forest has a rightful and a natural part, it has been the diplomatic business of their literature, not only to deny, at the expense of truth, the value of Mr. Wright's effort to their project's success, but to undo the tree-preserving popularity or expediency which he had created for his own park purpose. Not a hard task. "It took," said Mr. Wright to a man whom he saw felling a splendid elm, "the Almighty one hundred years to grow that tree, but any fool can cut it down in half an hour." And it took at least thirty years to build the park-taking expediency, that is in favor of a philanthropic object, but any diplomatic gnawing at its foundation, be it ever so little, if it is crafty, can undo it for one not so much so, in far less time. The architectural report, the instrument most effective in this undoing and which was not published till the prospective Metropolitan Park bill had reaped the advantage of the Forest Park expediency and its Commission that of our gifts in its behalf, in support of the woods destruction which it advises, says, "It follows that the notion that it would be wrong and even sacrilegious to suggest that this vegetation ought to be controlled and modified is a mistake." Perhaps so; but it is not one which Mr. Wright, in behalf of his Forest Park, ever made or suggested. And if to control and modify vegetation is a park necessity there is no reason why, to the infinitely lesser extent of the necessity, it could not be exercised in behalf of a forest park as of any other,—of "scenery" in which the woods is the main feature as of scenery in which it has little or no part. But from certain well-polished stones flung at the naturalists as "extremists" from another quarter of the same encampment, I judge the sentence given may be yet another missile, with characteristic diplomatic indirection, aimed at their devoted heads. Nor am I quite certain that its service has not still a third object. Under diplomatic rule, double purposes are as common as double'dealing. Be this as it may, the "mistake" which holds life sacred is one to which man owes no small debt. In the preservation of human life it is the divine ounce of prevention worth all the prison and gallows pounds of cure ever resorted to, and in that of the forest (where the destruction has a thousand temptations to one against human life, the life dependent upon its preservation) all the regulation axes. At any rate, it is to the resurrection of this all but dead and buried mistake that the Metropolitan Park system owes its existence, and, if it wants it, will have to owe its preservation or perpetuity.

The Metropolitan purpose, "the preservation of scenery," so apparently harmonious with the preservation of the Fells woods, was proved by the report to mean neither its preservation as under Nature's purpose and her own repairs it existed at the taking nor as protected in them it would exist, nor did it mean such preservation as "controlled and modified" by man it *might* exist: it meant as under such controlling and modifying for an *alien* purpose it would be forced to exist. Because its views or pictures had been damaged by fire, the browsing of animals, and the axe of the cord-wood dealer, in this report's estimation they are not as they stood "wild," but "artificial to a high degree," and, somewhat on the "bite of the same dog cure," their repairing must also in the highest degree be artificial,—again the axe of man. And because Nature in her struggle to make her own repairs cannot, against the odds of a constantly repeated axe destruction, fully restore her scenery in accordance with her own park design, a forest of seedling instead of as now partly stump-sproutage growth, it proceeds on the hypothesis that even given time and that other indispensable condition, protection and proper care, she would not through her own destructive and reproductive processes, or evolutions, consult among her trees the "survival of the fittest," and it recommends to the park management the gradual destruction of what it holds to be the unfit, the sprout growth. It says, "To restore beauty in such woods as are now dull and crop-like, large areas must be gradually cleared of sprout growth, selling the standing crop, subsequently killing the stumps, and encouraging seedling trees to take possession." "The mills of God grind slowly," but it is not necessary to take for granted that they do not grind surely, or that the meal would be longer in coming than with man at the crank. Stump sproutage is not immortal; and since, in justice to the present scenery and the present enjoyment thereof by the present public, the process in either case, not to be excessively ugly, must be *gradual*, why is not the scythe of old Father Time as good a regenerative instrument as the axe? In our own woods where the axe, except against the dead, has for nearly forty years been prohibited, it would seem so, for the seedling growth there has already gained upon the sproutage; and, notwithstanding the annual visitation of the infestation, until this past summer no woods was more vigorous or beautiful. Owing to causes which have their place in later pages, its share of suffering from the pest this year was greater than on any previous year. And even wholly under Nature's "controlling and modifying" would not our Fells be safer than, as now appears to be the case, wholly under that of an axe-wielding power without legal restraint as to either the character or amount of the tree destruction? While that power stands in so much greater need of it, it hardly seems fair that the controlling and modifying should be devoted so exclusively to the vegetation, nor with such the case can one feel quite as well assured of the "subsequent killing of the stumps" and the consequent seedling and scenic results as of the "selling of the standing crop" and their consequent financial or political gains. And the tree destruction is not by any means to be confined to stump sproutage, nor has the beautifying or bettering of the woods any great part in its object. The report says, "To prepare for *increasing* the interest and beauty of the scenery, work must be directed to removing screens of foliage, to opening vistas through 'notches,' to substituting low ground cover for high woods in many places," etc., and on an earlier page, "A ground covering of bushes will serve as well as grass when it is only a question of keeping a view open and there is no need of providing strolling places for crowds or smooth playgrounds for boys and children." If such benevolent provision as a rambling ground for crowds, forestal or otherwise, is anywhere in the Fells deemed a *necessity*, it does not appear in the report. The only question there is open views, and, when it is only a question of keeping them open the forest and its manifold benefits to *crowds* must stand aside. It says, "The beautiful variety and intricacy of this bushy growth is often, and indeed generally, remarkable and delightful. With time the bushes of sweet fern, bayberry, viburnum, and the like grow more and more numerous and entangled; and their combination with the dark cedars and the white birches often helps to form even broad landscape of rare beauty. Slowly, however, this type of landscape vanishes. From the midst, perhaps, of junipers which browsing cattle have avoided or from clumps of crowded bushes, slow-growing oaks and other forest trees start up from seeds brought by the winds, birds, or squirrels. Slowly, but surely, as the great trees grow in height and breadth, the low-growing birches, cedars, junipers, and bushes are overshadowed and, as it were, suffocated, and in the end the forest of seedling trees takes full possession.

"On the other hand it is obvious that the bushy stage of type is so beautiful in itself that it ought to be preserved in many places for itself alone; while it is equally obvious that in such parts of the reservations as command broad views which would be shut from sight by trees this bushy ground cover will need to be encouraged in every possible way, even, if need be, by going through the natural order of felling trees, killing the stumps, and pasturing the rough ground for a limited time."

And thus it will be seen that should the forest,—through *Nature's* processes, mark, *not* man's,—a victor over stump sproutage, *again* arise and, in the glory of its seedling growth and the "sublime audacity" of its persistence over generations of resistance, again plead its inalienable right to the Fells, it must *again* and yet *again* be fought down, that, if possible, Nature's own Fells design, a forest park, may at last be conquered. And it is not only in the "places" where the "bushy type" should be "preserved for itself alone" or in the low ground where "broad views would be shut from sight" that the woods must be sacrificed. The hills, the artistically, scientifically, and popularly acknowledged province of the woods, must also be forced to share in the sacrifice. Regardless of the fact that rough stone observatories would be an harmonious and enjoyable remedy for the evil, the summit trees must go down, for they would conceal the "broad prospect," so also, where they would hide fine "ledges and crags" —and where in the Fells would they not?—or partly hide them, must the lower trees. In short, in the Fells nowhere must Nature, to use Mr. Wright's expression in another connection, be allowed "to resume her work of covering and beautifying her own bones in her own way."

If the woods, as according to the report it is ultimately to exist, has any place in the Fells, it is not therein defined. You are indirectly permitted to infer that when it isn't in something's way it may possibly escape destruction, and that is all. Even the "open groves" which, if "pasturing is resumed and continued after well-spaced trees have been developed," are the "result," and which—as the Fells now exists, or did at the taking—"present, perhaps, the most lovely local scenery of the reservations," it would seem, are not *then* to be, for it is in these "open groves" that the "impractical and inappropriate" "pre-eminently 'park-like' type" consists. Taste is a matter, more or less, of education and association and scenic enjoyment, like all else the outcome of the soul and senses, is a matter of individual taste. My own accepts as beautiful scenery both when Nature operates alone and when art co-operates with her; but it must be co-operation, not an effort to so "control" her operations as ultimately to defeat her designs. She must still be mistress; and I don't agree with the report that under her own repairing her pictures are not "wild,"—those in the Fells certainly are,—and still less do I agree with it that her part stump-sproutage woods is "tame" or "tedious" or "monotonous," "crop-like," or anything else depreciative which in support of its destruction the report urges. The damages are "artificial," but the repairs are *not*, and the scenery is, therefore, wild; and, if it is "tame" or the rest of it anywhere, it is where the damage is so recent that the repairs have had no time to produce results. Where they *have*, the scenery is exceedingly picturesque, or if it is not you wouldn't know it unless you read the report. In Mr. Wright's time hundreds, artists among them, testified to its beauty; and, as for stump-sprout growth, I would decidedly, if not respectfully, recommend giving it, as long as it lasts, at least a fair chance with the seedling. Such growth is much in keeping with the rough, toss-and-tumble character of the Fells woods. Where some vigorous old stump has had time and the hardihood to send aloft a couple or more of giant trees, its presence among the different tree combinations of the constantly varying rocky woods levels is exceedingly fascinating. In our own woods the rugged majesty of some of these is enough to make a stone shout; and certainly the rocks, ledges, and crags *there* cry out, not for their destruction, but against it. Nor is the Fells woods interior without its vistas, its openings to its open views. The secret of Nature's charm, whether her scenery be close or open, is still that she does not and cannot reveal all at once, and in the woods these only half-revealed views tempt the rambler to further and further invigorating exploration, nor is his effort unrewarded; for at every step not only do the interior pictures blend harmoniously one into another, but a thousand forestal attractions meet his eyes. Infinite are the dells, mossy nooks, fern-covered plateaus, the rock-work, overhanging crags, the brooks, the cascades; and in time, worn by eager feet alone, there would be a thousand winding paths, each one a vista to views beyond, sometimes the open ones and sometimes those of the woods. But plead, poor Fells. Even though after thirty years of appeal your woods still stands on the auction block, it is not yet all bid off. Speak, then, while you may.

What I shall now submit, historical and otherwise, was written earlier than the foregoing, and before I had read the report; for, though presented to me by my brother—who had also then not read it—at the time of its publication, it did not until some weeks ago, occur to me to give it attention, and I, show myself, therefore, at a loss to account for a tree destruction reports of which, as well as the sound of the axe in my own neighborhood, from time to time reached me. Taking, as I did, for granted that, whatsoever the means of preservation, the term "preservation of scenery" would include the Fells woods with its open views, at least to the extent in which both existed at the time of the securing,— in other words, that preservation meant preservation, not creation,—it did not seem necessary to inform myself further. Nor, although I told them my gift was in behalf of my father's woods-preserving hope, did it seem at all necessary to the Commissioners in accepting it to so inform me. Even the writer of the report, though behind the diplomatic scenes and probably a principal actor in them, must have found that phrase somewhat equivocal; for after thus explaining it, "The purpose of investing public money in the purchase of the several Metropolitan reservations was to secure for the enjoyment of present and future generations such interesting and beautiful scenery as the lands acquired can supply," he adds, "at all events, it is on the assumption that this was the purpose in view that the following report, with the investigation it describes, is based."

HISTORICAL SKETCH.

No man, however gifted, sets his pen to work for right against might or Mammon with any great chance of becoming anything but poorer. And in 1839, after seven crowded years of such work in the anti-slavery cause, two events occurred which brought Mr. Wright so near destitution that for many years his life was a hand-to-hand fight with the wolf at the door. In 1837, while Secretary of the American Anti-slavery Society in New York, he chanced, at De Behr's repository of foreign books, to come upon a cheap copy of La Fontaine's Fables in the French, with some two hundred woodcuts in it. His little son, he tells us in his introduction to his translations, was just "beginning to feel the intellectual magnetism of pictures," and, to please him, he bought the book. The pictures alone, however, were not enough to satisfy the child. He must have the stories, too. And from putting them into English by word of mouth the father became as fascinated as the son, and, finding no English version, "resolved to cheat sleep of an hour every morning till there should be one." A year later, at the call of the "political action" abolitionists, of which he was one, he left the national society to become the editor in Boston of the *Massachusetts Abolitionist*, the State organ of his party. The success of political action to him depended upon the nomination and strong united support of men whose *own* actions proved their anti-slavery principles beyond doubt. In explanation of this position he wrote in 1849:—

As editor I felt it my duty to advocate an entire separation from the political parties, and in the use of the suffrage in full accordance with these principles. Though this ground is now occupied by all the abolitionists of the United States except a few leaders in what is called non-resistance or no governmentism,—the distinct anti-slavery vote having risen from less than 7,000 in 1840, to 57,000 in 1843,—they were then so far from it that even the committee under which I acted did not feel sustained in employing me another year.

As the committee were poor as well as prudent, they were also unsustained in paying him fully for the first. In this strait the publication of fables, the music and merit of which had so beset him in his translating as to turn his task into the most irresistible of pleasures, did not seem so forlorn a hope or an investment so unpromising, and under the encouragement of his generous and well-to-do brother-in-law, who was ready to advance him the necessary funds, he ventured upon the undertaking, doing editorial work for antislavery papers in the mean while, and importing for his translations the expensive and speaking illustrations of Grandville. While the publication was in process, his brother-in-law failed; and there was nothing for Mr. Wright to do but to take his book from door to door, and true to his own lines on "Hope,"

> "When plans are wrecked and fail,
>   I'll brush away the tear,
>   Hoist up another sail
>   And by thy light-house steer."

That was what he did, going from city to city, first in this country and then in England and Scotland. It took three desperate, courageous years, but the edition was at last sold, and his debt or debts—for debt necessitates debt—at last paid. Not wholly from his sales, but from them and later earnings.

It was while pushing this cruelly slow work in London that Mr. Wright first realized the necessity of parks to crowded and growing cities. Those of London, after her stifled, starving, begging, and thieving poverty, must have come upon him like heaven after hades, and must have been some compensation for the impulses of benevolence he had hourly to cheat.

Despite his efforts to cheer and be cheered, a number of such pathetic passages as the following force their way among the graphic and humorous descriptions of his letters home:—

There are many sights here to make one's heart ache. Vice undergoing its awful penalties, and, what is harder, virtuous industry begging for both work and bread. How often did I wish I could live my life over again. Surely I would keep out of debt, that I might neither be banished from my own family, nor have to deny myself the luxury of now and then giving a crumb to help others. . . . Often do I see some poor wretched mother with four or five children, one not bigger than Kate, asking charity in the street. They make me think of my little deserted brood. . . . There is beggary enough to break one's heart, unless it be made a thousand times tougher than yours or mine; and pride that would provoke a saint to desperation,—much more me who am not a saint. But I shall be away from it I trust, and not be quite so miserable as to be with it and not be able to relieve it.

In England Mr. Wright kept sharp watch on all from which he could get knowledge or inspiration. He did not mean that a "sojourn abroad" at such dear cost as his own should be a moment of it wasted. His "Gropings in Great Britain," published in his *Chronotype* in 1846, deal with much that he investigated, and contain four papers on London's parks. He says of them:—

Royalty has cost too much not to have been good for something. London owes to it her magnificent parks. She would go crazy without them. They are large tracts of territory which royalty reserved to itself for its own purposes in the neighborhood of the city when it was not so large. They have long since been grown into it, and are for the delight and recreation of the whole people, under the regulations of Her Majesty's Commissioners of Woods and Forests.

Describing St. James Park, he says:—

Here opens upon you the magnificence of London, the glory of the aristocracy and the pride of royalty. Here at one end, is the home of the mighty captains of the land and sea forces, that conquer the world and keep it conquered in our day, and the Midas lords who create the wealth to do it with; at the other end is the Queen's home, Buckingham palace. . . . Yet shaded as this park is by power, nobility and royalty, it is the people's own park. Here they throng with no fear of being run over by noblemen's carriages.

Hyde Park he calls "the great rabble park of London, where on Sundays the poor from sunless alleys roll on the grass and get their sunning for a whole week."

The flowers are not pulled [he says] nor the trees injured, though they are perfectly accessible to the crowd. In all the beautiful points of view, and such points are numerous, there are seats. Buckingham palace, seen from the sandy desert of an esplanade before it, is an ugly and forbidding pile of stone, but seen through the vista of trees from the park, it is exceedingly beautiful and imposing. What a pity, did I a thousand times think it, that republicanism cannot afford the sovereign people just such a park without the sight of the palace. In any city of 100,000 people, such a park would about double their happiness, young and old.

Elsewhere he says of Hyde Park, "I shouldn't wonder if this great national park acted on thousands of Londoners like a chain, binding them to the city in preference to other homes." And in his Groping "On London Squares," he says:—

But I was going to speak of the parks, and I have not yet said half that should be said of the squares. They are the noses and the parks the lungs of London. They suggest considerations that are of the utmost importance to the destinies of cities. London it is well known is one of the healthiest of cities, far more so than Liverpool, Manchester, or Glasgow. Whether its squares and parks contribute to this, is a question that I leave others to discuss. But if happiness contributes to health there can be no doubt they have much to do with it.

His "Gropings," "Poverty in London" and "The Middle Classes," could I but copy them wholly, would give a realizing sense of the enormity of the masses needing daily and hourly, soul and body, of their parks, what otherwise they have not the means to obtain, the pure and restful influence of nature; but in the following the keynote of his work for the Fells sounds again and perhaps clearer than in what I have given:—

No stranger [he writes] in studying London should take Hyde Park first. Before he sees it he should have threaded the sunless streets and rat-hole alleys that pervade the masses of brick and mortar in the ancient city. He should have seen the Seven Dials, Saffron Hill and Field Lane, Rag Fair and Printing House Square. He should have taken a circuit through Spitalfield, perambulated the East End of London Docks, passed under the Thames, and come up by the by streets of Southwark. After having had this surfeit of brick and mortar, let him come abruptly for the first time upon Hyde Park, out of the confused mass of grandeur and meanness which lies south of it. He will be astonished. Let him walk an hour or two in this great national promenade, and he will be still more astonished. In five minutes he may enter a deep forest, where no grass grows, and the dry leaves of last year rustle under his feet, and primeval nature still reigns in solitude. From this wilderness he may come upon a small lake where the water fowl breed undisturbed. All this in the heart of swarming London.

When a law which to any degree meets the people's needs bids fair to succeed, it seldom escapes a crippling amendment. And such an amendment by a division of control in the Medford Fells parted that which "God had joined," the water supply and park interests, and also deprived the park of a large acreage of its natural and still wild boundary, the argument for the last being Medford's "building interests." Before visiting the present smaller Fells Reservation, one needs only to go through the "swarming" present "Greater Boston's" brick and mortar to appreciate not only the mocking satire of such an argument, but the need of the greater ells Park urged by Mr. Wright in these Appeals. Of course, if only the caterpillars and the other tree-killers, the official ones, will leave off destroying it, what Fells we have is son.ething to be eternally—or even, if must be, temporarily—grateful for. But not the less would the metropolis have been the gainer, could there have been ceded to her at least twenty thousand more health and heart inspiring acres; and for the instigator of that amendment, living as he does in paradisal groves and with the "open sesame" to Nature everywhere in his purse, to grudge poorer people that exempted Fells argues meanness greater than even his means. No other Fells owner had so rare an opportunity to do a generous public-spirited act; but little did he care for the "greatest good to the greatest number," or, if the price paid him to get back a small but indispensable portion of that exempted boundary has anything to say, to any number except number one. In 1884 Mr. Wright said of him, "The only opponent I have ever found to the public domain project, and he is, perhaps, the largest proprietor of territory in the Fells, says to me, 'It is a good thing.' He only objects to my method of realizing it. I have put the price too low, estimating it at only what the territory is assessed at for taxes."

This "only opponent" to the only method by which the greater Fells could have been realized to the Greater Boston, whatever objection he may have had as "the largest Fells proprietor" to too low a price, seems not to have had any as a land purchaser, for after Mr. Wright's death, scenting in the air the park success his labors had insured, he was on hand, or said to be, with a local park scheme of his own, one probably in behalf of his "building interests," and certainly to be realized by a method of his own. And in this enterprise he made through an agent application for Fells land, and among others to two, if not more, of the owners who had pledged land to the success of Mr. Wright's method, and to these he urged as a reason for "too low a price" in his case, not his own park scheme, but the "park interest," and his own greater ability to hold lands in its favor. With one of the two, to his disadvantage and later indignation, he was successful, but by the other he was told that with the "park interest" the *object* he could himself hold the land. Little wonder that in getting my petition for the Metropolitan Park law, a number to whom I presented it were surprised not to see this apparently no longer opponent's name on my lists. And, when I told one gentleman I had applied for it in vain, he said, "Give me your paper and I'll get it." And, if his exempted Fells land was any part of this park interest effort, little wonder he said of Mr. Wright's object, "It is a good thing," and still less that Mr. H. W. S. Cleveland, who with a party of others visited the Fells in 1857, should in giving his own word for its taking have urged the "dangers of delay."

With the amendment Mr. De Las Casas's diplomacy thus deals: "This bill with slight amendment was enacted as Chapter 407 of the Acts of 1893, and has been amended from time to time as necessities have arisen." One of these necessities practically, if not legally, was the necessity of amending the amendment in behalf of something like the "unitary" park "control" which Mr. Wright had urged, and against the neglect of which *his* law and method was especially guarded. To secure it piecemeal, he once assured me, would be to invite—just what happened under the Metropolitan method— the greed of speculators and private owners. Whether under that method opposition to the amendment would have killed the bill or not is something which neither its advocates nor I can know, as it was not tried. But this we know: the people in their neglect of Mr. Wright's ounce of prevention have had to pay a heavy pound of cure. Not that their present park is not worth it every cent and more. To me it is worth any cost except such cost as threatens its defeat.

Mr. Wright's discovery of the Fells was not till 1864, when

he came to live in Medford, and until 1880 his time was still pressed with other important reform work, but he did not forget the city's need of a park. His *Chronotype* kept watch over the people's rights in their Common and Public Garden, which last he was the means of rescuing from a scheme in the "building" or some other private dollar interest which at one time threatened to destroy it. And think what a little heaven upon earth it is now. From the *Chronotype* of Sept. 7, 1847, I copy the following:—

A PUBLIC PROMENADE.—One of the evening papers of yesterday very properly commended the city of Roxbury for making provision for a rural cemetery of sixty acres, similar to Mount Auburn. Alluding to the good economy of the undertaking, it says, "Mount Auburn has paid for itself and left a surplus of thirty thousand dollars in the hands of the managers, and not a quarter of the land has yet been disposed of." It might be worth while to inquire whether this prosperity might not be well applied to make this famous cemetery more democratic, and give there a resting place for the poor as well as the rich clay. . Regard being had to the living we think no further burial ought to be allowed in the city on any consideration, but that provision for rural sepulture should be made for all. However, as we do not live for the purpose of dying, it is the object of our present article to inquire if some better provision cannot be made for the comfort of the living in regard to rural enjoyment. All prefer to sleep the long sleep under the green woods, and some of us would like to breathe the fresh air while we live oftener than we do. Since the great rural burying-ground has succeeded so well, why may we not have a great rural playground where we may snuff the fresh breezes, and sport with the green tresses of Nature without trespassing on deeded acres? London has its Greenwich, and we do not know how many other fine parks, in which its population expand free from city smoke and dust. These parks, though from seven to twenty miles out of town, are reached for a trifling sum by steamer or rail cars, and when reached have all the attractions which belong to the common idea of paradise,—fine green lawns, airy hills, densely wooded hillsides, mimic lakes covered with waterfowl, smooth, winding gravel walks, parterres of flowers, and rare trees, vine-clad arbors and mossy temples, and overreaching vistas of elms. Why cannot our city, in which our Common will soon be the only open patch of green worth mentioning, secure its future population and its present, too, a mile square park from five to ten miles from town, accessible in a few minutes by steam? There are grand seats which might be purchased for a mere song now, and the fitting up would cost but little, for nature is what we want to get at.

A fine park might be had in one or two places on our harbor, open to the sea breeze. A better one could be had by purchasing the noble Blue Hills in Milton, from which the State takes its name. A whole mountain for a playground— only think of it! Its susceptibility of improvement and embellishment would be infinite, without at all interfering with its sublime natural beauties. Twenty or thirty miles of easy graded corkscrew road up its side, and a crown of gardens and arbors on its top, would make it one of the first resorts for a sultry day in the world. The shady nooks and dells around its base would furnish admirable accommodation for picnic parties, and the exercise of going up and down its steeps would give, in the aggregate, ages and ages of life to our city population. And as we have a boasting propensity, we might make as much of it in that way as Edinburgh does of Arthur's Seat. Surely it would be no small thing if a citizen of Boston could of a sultry afternoon for a quarter of a dollar get transported a dozen miles and back, having ascended in the meantime seven hundred and odd feet and enjoyed one of the finest views in the world. And all this might be done by the united effort of the city.

In 1864, in Medford, with his home under Pine Hill, and from its top rock a glimpse of the city and ocean, and on all sides rocks, dells, hills, and the almost unbroken woods, another seat, near Boston, richer and more varied in its "sublime natural beauties," and needing no improvement and embellishment,—only that its larger promise of a future forest might be regarded in the preservation of its trees and their contiguity,—had revealed itself in the "old five-mile woods," or "Middlesex Fells." Loving the trees and humanity, and knowing the interdependence of each with each, it is little wonder Mr. Wright should soon have made himself master of the extent and resources of this great waste and wasted region, or that he should have seen in it the grandest possible future park of Boston, or later should have made its cause his own. There it lay, a magnificent forest gem or germ of four thousand acres in a setting of five municipalities, of which his "Park of the Future," written in 1877, says:—

The tract was left in the shape of a nearly circular basin rimmed with hills, which here and there rise above the top of Bunker Hill monument. Only two or three valleys break the contiguity. The interior of the basin is so rugged that our rugged ancestors, after checkering it all over with their characteristic stone fences, and planting apple trees which seem to find soil where little is visible to the naked eye, gave it up in despair, and let Nature resume her work of covering and beautifying her own bones in her own way. Now you find the old apple trees, or their descendants, struggling for breath in groves of forests where Doré would revel. . . . The entire tract is forever proof against any land speculation, for streets in it cannot run at right angles or any angles. Nothing but beauty in all sorts of curves is predestined there. Division and subdivision are laughed to scorn. The fantastic rock-ribbed basin is decreed by the nature of things to remain whole —a sort of oasis in a desert of vulgar cultivation—till art condescends to become a handmaid to Nature, and decorate it for the enjoyment of all the people.

Whatever dynamite, under the "Almighty Dollar" of the few against the many, might ultimately have done in defeat of a predestination so helpful to the many, it had done little in 1864. Indeed, so beneficial practically was Mr. Wright's tree-preserving influence that it had not done much during his life; and had the Fells been taken by his plan and law of 1882, as a little study of both in these Appeals will show, our park would have been considerably larger and far better secured to perpetuity, as well secured as in the nature or human nature of things it is possible for a park to be. In 1864 it was that Mr. Wright made his first attempt for his Fells park. And, though too true a man to adopt any of the corrupt practices of its diplomatic policy, he made it through the city government. All undaunted—if he had ever heard of it—by Mr. G. S. Hillard's remark to Mr. Cleveland on the occasion mentioned, that "you might as well try to persuade the Common Council to buy land in the moon as in the Fells," his first appeal was to that very council. But Mr. De Las Casas says of him, "He does not seem to have had a clear idea of the machinery by which his object could be accomplished." (By what follows I take "machinery" to mean governmental action. It could hardly have meant the practices of politicians by which the government, itself a political institution, is influenced; for he says also that "Mr. Wright was trained to his line of thought by association with the anti-slavery movement," and if he does not know what reason, *practically*, the pioneer abolitionists had to know these *practices*, he got his history lessons to very little purpose.) "For," he continues, "he figures out the great number of passengers who might be carried to them [the Fells], and on a basis of a profit thus assured urged the railroads to acquire them as a park to be called 'Mt. Andrew Park.'"

If you will consult City Document 123, you will find that Mt. Andrew Park was one of the papers read by Mr. Wright in his hearing before a committee of the City Council in behalf of securing the Fells as a park for Boston; and if you will turn to Mt. Andrew Park itself, the first of these Appeals, you will read: "But the cost! that is not the material question. The true question is will it pay?" And in what follows you will see that Mr. Wright's figures are cited solely to show that it will, and that it is the city, not the railroads, he urges to secure the Fells. His words are, "Mt. Andrew Park will pay. It may take a keen-sighted corporation to see it at first. But it only waits for the waking up of the people to their own right and interests to make it their common property, *both the park and the cheap road to it.*"

To prove his case, Mr. De Las Casas would of course have to invent his facts, and another untrue and depreciating assertion, congenial alike to wealthy caste politicians who have never forgiven Mr. Wright his share in the practical success of Afro-American emancipation, the favor of whom it might not be amiss to gain, and to such of his co-operation as would gladly see the fault of his so-called failure laid to anything except its real cause, was that "naturally he began to agitate and seek the assistance of those with whom he had worked in the anti-slavery cause." The only assistance Mr. Wright sought or had to seek was money help and the help of the politicians. The men of soul came of their own accord, and, in so far as they were his anti-slavery co-workers, consisted of his three lifelong personal friends, Whittier, Weld, and Sewall; and, unless the *dead* act, there could not have been another man. But the seeming support of the letters of the two first, in response to Mr. Wright's invitation to share with him the pleasures of one of his Forest Festivals,—letters which, proud of their humane and literary force, I published in my old sketch,—to his purpose was, perhaps, too much for Mr. De Las Casas's power of resistance. His statement that "Mr. Wright was trained to his line of thought by association with the anti-slavery movement" was, however, far from an untruth. He certainly was so trained, and he certainly did apply the knowledge of such training to his Fells cause. Before a single grain of anti-slavery manhood could be inoculated into administrative halls anywhere, he and his co-workers had learned that in the very teeth of a governmentally supported and encouraged mob martyrdom they must arouse among the unprejudiced a demand for justice to the black man and his rights, and before the Fells could hope for governmental action he knew a like rousing process as to its park claims and the people's right to it and need for it must also be gone through. If he had not known it, the legislative sequel to his City Council hearings would have taught it to him. Machinery, whether human or otherwise, must have motive power as well as an engine, fire or fervor. Oiling alone won't stir it. And what Mr. De las Casas doesn't seem to have a clear idea of is that the pro-park steam, or popularity, generated by Mr. Wright, and of which his *plan of securing* was a necessary and effective instrument, had anything practically to do with the later success. When Sylvester Baxter said, in his "Park Guide," of this steam, "The public sentiment aroused by this agitation finally led to the Metropolitan success," he was not writing politics, but history. As the park cause is, or ought to be, more largely the people's cause than the government's, it is moral and philanthropic steam I speak of. With the Mammon steam, or incentive, the administrative engines are only too disastrously overcharged, so disastrously that but for a little counter-engineering by reformers their nations would soon be run to complete destruction. And Mr. Wright's machinery being the human and the will of the people persistently asserted, a part of it was of course the administrative, and the same as that of the later movers. The difference lies in the two activities alone. While Mr. Wright's recognized the possibilities of administrative achievement through moral means, the other doesn't appear to have done so.

Mr. De Las Casas further says that "practical philanthropists like Converse"—whose name be blessed—"and public men like Long and Loring lent their aid in one way and another; but the desired result did not come." It did not by Mr. Wright's plan, the worse for the Fells and the people; but the fault and the failure there was due to no lacking on Mr. Wright's part, practical or otherwise. The public men were not practical philanthropists like Converse, but practical politicians, a class of men who never do anything till a cause has been made popular, and never then at the cost of their own purses, but that of the public. And now, if you will follow historically the City Council drama, you will see why Mr. Wright devised his plan of action as he did, and why it was a necessity to any park success.

The hearings before the City Council Committee took place in 1869. The figures of Mr. Wright's "Mt. Andrew Park," proving the financial value of his object to Boston, were not the only or the most important of his figures. In another paper read at a later hearing, and in which he argued the great necessity of healthful country homes for the families of city laborers, he had figures to show that in Boston's county the chance at that time of being born dead was a little more than three times as great as in any other part of Massachusetts, and that the chance of dying in the first year of life in the same county to that out of it was as fourteen to ten.

The chances of dying before you reach the age of five, he said, are vastly greater in the city than out of it; that is, out of Boston in Massachusetts, including all the other cities, some of which are quite dense. If I were making a comparison between Suffolk county and the average country towns, or such towns as lie within ten miles of Boston, you would find the disparity of these ratios still further exaggerated. [And yet in the face of the fact that the present "Greater Boston" has a *smaller* Fells acreage, the present park management are only too ready to cut down instead of caring for its fewer trees, the producers of the much-needed pure air.] What I say is that it is criminal to breed the human race in Boston. With all your breathing places, it is criminal. And if there is any force in the universe above us, it will hold you to account for it. I say that with the blessed inventions of Watt and Stephenson we can command for our laboring population breathing air fit to breed the human race in out of Boston.

And his paper concludes with:—

I have advocated this park, because I think it will lead to this result. I am happy to see that the city is advised to buy something more than a pleasure ground. I know, gentlemen, that I have presented to you a location which will carry out these views. And I have said to you and demonstrated to you that it will cost the city not a cent. It may require an outlay of capital, but there is no risk, there is no cost. You have it all free. Providence has put it in your hands for nothing, and I defy any civil engineer to say me no.

Of the General Court action which, in 1870, was the outcome of these hearings, Mr. Wright in his "Appeal" called "The Park Question," page 9, wrote:—

The well-guarded park bill of last year which submitted the whole problem of the future beauty and grandeur of our city to a competent and impartial commission was defeated in the interest of projectors who have manifest private ends to serve. Everybody has private ends, and the public is not about to forego its own ends lest somebody should be privately benefited by it. It ought and it will do the best it can for its whole self without injury to any individual, and if any individual is enriched by it so much the better for him or her. Let us have fair play and no dog in the manger.

The report of the City Commission proved its impartiality, and the papers, of which there were a large number, were strongly and ably in favor of a park or parks. But since the Fells was the only easily and cheaply accessible location then urged that had anything like the extent of territory, woods, rocks, waters, and other requisites for the city's future beauty and grandeur, "Mt. Andrew Park" alone offered the city problem a solution. With a proviso 17 by which, as a law, it couldn't take effect without a two-thirds vote of the city's legal voters, the bill passed, and by its failure to get the vote was defeated. This law, Section 4, empowered Boston to locate her park or parks "in or near her city limits." And significant of private end projectors, and of the dog in the manger spirit, the "majority vote," with which its Section 17 had started life, had been raised, by amendment, to that two-thirds vote. And *more* significant, in 1875, with a Section 17 allowing to it the majority vote denied the earlier law, another law—or the same revised—was successfully passed, the Section 3 of which empowered Boston to locate her park or parks within *her own limits* only, and which, by empowering other municipalities to do the same, covered not only its own meanness in a device by which Boston was to gain possible park benefits at the cost of localities needing them less, but the more niggardly fact that in shutting out of unitary control park locations under distinct jurisdictions it had closed the door in the face of the Fells and Blue Hills, Boston's only chance of parks with forest contiguity, the indispensable means in every healthful and happy way to her growth, present and future.

If grist is too large, it may not be other than practical common sense to enlarge the mill; and finding his cause quite as far outside of the city limit as to wisdom and philanthropy, at *this* period, as he later found it outside that of *private generosity*, Mr. Wright set about increasing both; in other words, he set about manufacturing the practicality of his object, and, as administrative generosity is the result of private generosity, he began on private generosity. From time to time he issued public invitation to the people at large to visit the Fells, offering himself to act as guide. He kept the subject alive through the papers, taking care to stimulate all the interests awakened, pro and con, and before long a number of able writers had come to his aid. I regret that in putting together these "Appeals" I had on hand only a portion of what he had written. His lectures, too, are a number of them missing, and one published is incomplete.

Mr. Wright's literary and mathematical powers at this epoch had so far got the better of his poverty that he was enabled, during the years from 1870 to 1880, to purchase the woods of his own contribution. Hoping to encourage similar action of interest among Fells owners, he wrote in 1877:—

Once let the people of Boston see what Nature has done for the site of which I speak, and how enjoyable it is, and the only danger would be that they would be taxing themselves to buy it and would foolishly deprive the proprietors of the opportunity of doing the wise and politic thing—for I don't pretend it would be generous—of giving it to them. When I speak of giving, I speak as one of the proprietors, for I live on the hither brim of the basin, and I should be glad to make a present of fifty or sixty acres, a tract which for value and beauty of its forest growth, and the grandeur of its outlook, I think is equal to that of any other tract of the same size that would be included in the park. If any of the other proprietors are similarly minded, I shall be glad to hear from them.

During this ten years of effort for the Fells, in addition to labors which hardly gave him time for a long breath, Mr. Wright hoped that younger men, and men who, though good, were not so strongly identified with unpopular good causes as to have incurred the enmity of the ruling Mammon powers, would take the matter up. But no independent effort was made, and in 1880 he put his own wits to work.

His hearing before the City Council was twelve years later than the day of Mr. Cleveland's urging, and yet, in 1880, Mr. Hillard's governmental hopelessness must still have been true, for before the more practical Metropolitan movers ventured into the legislature twenty-four years had been added to the twelve. In 1880, then, the situation would seem to demand a measure by which without further loss or delay it *would* be practicable for the people, if they had the sense, by their own effort and generosity to secure their Fells for themselves, and which, should they fail in so doing, would by its social and educational character have overcome that governmental hopelessness. At any rate Mr. Wright meant that nothing he could do should be wanting in furtherance of this twofold aim. His plan proposed to secure the Fells by a two-thirds vote and appropriation from the municipalities, and to encourage this vote it called for a voluntary contribution sufficient to extinguish private titles, which at the appraised value of that date he found to aggregate about $300,000. The contribution took the form of a pledge the payment of which was conditional upon the vote being favorable. It was a contribution in which he meant Boston to share in proportion to her benefits, if not her wealth. The Forestry Law, Chapter 255, which he caused to be passed in its behalf, vested the title of the Fells Park in the Commonwealth, and the park was to be held by the Board of Agriculture acting as a Board of Forestry, in perpetuity for the benefit of the municipalities in which it was situated.

On Oct. 15, 1880, Mr. Wright called together some two hundred people, and on Bear Hill in the Stoneham Fells formed a small association to devise plans and to discuss the means of carrying out any one that might be agreed upon. Two plans were sketched, Mr. Wright's and that of Mr. Wilson Flagg, who years before Mr. Wright's discovery had plead the Fells cause and made his own successless appeal to a selfish and short-sighted government in behalf of its salvation as a forest conservatory,—a wild natural garden for the indigenous fauna and flora and for purposes of science and natural history. Mr. Wright's plan might well be made to embrace this distinct and yet harmonious feature, and was the one adopted. During the next two months these able advocates had made such headway in popularizing their project that the mass meeting held in Medford Jan. 1, 1881, was crowded and addressed by speakers who, having just returned from a smart drive through the Fells, were strong for action in its favor. 1881, later on, was the year of the Ravine Woods desecration, and this disastrous tree destruction Mr. Wright tried hard to prevent; but the proprietor of the woods, in an attempt to take advantage of his public spirit, charged a price beyond what could be hoped for from any other source, and far beyond Mr.

Wright's ability to pay for in the prescribed time, although he and another were ready with $1,000 each from their own purses, to get subscribed.

The letters written Mr. Wright in this transaction had their place in one of these "Appeals," but, after being put in type, were, by the request of one of the later movers, excluded as not helpful to the law. And in Mr. De Las Casas's sketch the blame of the Ravine Wood destruction, as another offering at the diplomatic shrine, is laid to "speculators," not its proprietors. The letters read:—

BOSTON, March 8, 1881.

ELIZUR WRIGHT, ESQ.

Dear Sir,—I have been thinking for some time of cutting the timber off my land on Ravine Street, near Spot Pond; but I have been told or requested not to do so until I see you, as I learn you are making an effort to buy the whole territory. But as I have about 900,000 feet of lumber I wish to put into money, I had about determined to cut it. If you desire to see me, please do so at once, above address.

Yours,
J. B. BUTTERFIELD, per F.

BOSTON, March 10, 1881.

ELIZUR WRIGHT, ESQ.

Dear Sir,—If I *sell*, I want to make a clean sale of the thirty-two acres, timber and land. My price is $18,000. But for and under the circumstances will sell it for $17,000 (seventeen thousand dollars) cash, if accepted very soon. I can get $12,000 out of the timber alone.

Yours truly,
JOHN B. BUTTERFIELD, per G. F. B.

BOSTON, March 14, 1881.

ELIZUR WRIGHT, ESQ.

Dear Sir,—Yours at hand and noted. The lot stands me in *over* $18,000 in cash, and I think my price reasonable. But as I stated to you when here, I have a use for the money that I *can* realize out of the timber. I can thribble my investment before the close of the year, and I have decided to sacrifice the *beauty* of the place for the necessity of the case; and have a contract ready for signature now. It was only by accident I happened to hear of you, and requested to write to you.

    Yours very truly,
      G. F. BUTTERFIELD for JOHN B. BUTTERFIELD.

P.S.—The place is mortgaged for $8,000, and formerly had $9,500 on it.

Mr. Wright in publishing them (Boston *Daily Advertiser*) says:—

In reply to the first I asked him his lowest price, and in reply to the second I felt obliged to say to him that I thought he rated the commercial value of his property too high. It is assessed at $12,000. I have no doubt that its æsthetic and hygienic values are quite up to that. But I advised him to spare the trees as more profitable than the cutting. The friends of the project can judge for themselves, from Mr. Butterfield's third letter, how it affects the situation.

He also said:—

The proprietor is an entire stranger to me, and I would not hurt his feelings for the world. I hope I shall not by publishing his three letters.

He might have spared himself this concern. The gentleman's feelings at seeing his letters in print could hardly have been other than those of gratification. Devotion to "financial value" and pride in wealth rather than in worth has been too well proved by our course against the Filipino to leave room for doubt.

A tree with Mr. Wright was something almost human and wholly divine, and in no other part of his Fells had God blessed a spot with trees older and grander than in the Ravine Woods. "Possibly," he writes in an "Appeal" of 1884, "those health-giving trees were destined to be sacrificed to save their race.

If Boston could see them as they lie there, tears would flow if not dollars." And he determined it should be no fault of his if they did not, at least, prove the saviors of their own little Fells brotherhood. By 1882 he had obtained in his Forestry Law all the legislation necessary to his plan and the taking of lands in behalf of forests or parks anywhere in Massachusetts, and had enlisted trustees to take charge of the conditional obligations. This done, the object of his labors was to direct as broad a public attention as possible to the fact that the way was now open to secure the Fells, the practical success of which lay within the power of the people themselves, as under an honest policy it would lay in all that concerns them. He did this through the press by the strengthened argument, science, wit, earnestness, and frequency of his appeals, and socially by a series of yearly "Forest Festivals" held in different parts of his Fells, that the speaking, which it was his care to procure might be supplemented by its different attractions, and that his trees, "most eloquent in the golden silence of their sunlit boughs," might still help to plead his cause and their own.

His Fells as a park glorious among the parks of nations, while it failed to stimulate in the wealthy the private generosity and public spirit he would gladly have aroused, did not fail to excite their pride and ambition, and the spring of 1883 had hardly begun before his words, "Everybody seems to be enthusiastically in favor of having the thing done at the expense of somebody else," had become the truth. In other words, the Fells or park popularity, including the favor of the wealthy so indispensable to administrative action, had become an established fact. How well established I have some reason to know, for hoping to help a little myself, as well as save Mr. Wright some of the many expenses—printing, map-making, barge-hiring, advertising, etc.—which he so constantly and gladly met from his own purse, I undertook to conduct an entertainment in each of the Fells municipalities and in Boston;

and in seeking the co-operation of other ladies, out of the many calls I made, palace or cottage, not a door was closed against me. "For the Fells" on my card was "open sesame" enough, and I left no house without its "God speed" to Mr. Wright's noble purpose.

Mr. De Las Casas, after saying that about "practical philanthropists," etc., continues with:—

and Mr. Wright wrote sadly in 1883: "The people must move and act spontaneously if anything is to be done. It is everybody's axe; and unless everybody grinds it, it will be dull for generations to come. The wood-choppers are sure to grind theirs while a tree is left. Here is work for the press, the pulpit, the platform—for everybody who likes to breathe good air, drink pure water, and see green things."

Now, although he may have spoken sadly at this epoch, he was very far from abandoning his effort either for the success of his own plan or its object.

"Men failed, betrayed him, but his zeal seemed nourished
    By failure and by fall;
Still a large faith in human kind he cherished,
    And in God's love for all."

Knowing the greater worth of his own plan, he meant what few years of life might be left should be given to it. But he did not fail to encourage other plans. In 1884 he wrote in answer to a statement of some of the difficulties of his undertaking: "They are doubtless considerable, but not insurmountable. The plan presented may be impracticable, but other plans are possible, and there is always a practicable plan for everything that is desirable." In 1883, when he wrote the passage, "The people must move and act spontaneously," he prefaced it with "there will be no begging." Generous men have a larger faith in generosity than selfish ones, and until 1884 he hoped none might be necessary, his conditional papers in the hands of his trustees being publicly announced. But, finding "what's everybody's business is nobody's" too ungenerously true in his case, he determined his plan should have the benefit of canvassers, and at once began the work of organizing Public Domain Clubs in the Fells municipalities and in Boston, which, acting under the Fells Association, might elect committees and employ them. Such a club, comprising two hundred members, he organized in Medford. But it needed that some ten or twenty others as enterprising and as ready to work for nothing as himself should, without his aid or prompting, take hold with him. And his last Forest Festival, in 1885, had for its object to so strengthen his little Fells Association as to aid him in influencing this help. In 1885, too, by his invitation, the National Forestry Congress was held in Boston. Towards its success, and still that of his Fells, with always the added hope of encouraging what favor he might for the establishment of similar forest parks near other large cities, he did all he could. This was in September, and, feeling his strength lessen, his work till the morning of his death was to see men who, after it, might be willing, if not to adopt his plan, to take up his cause. And on November 21 he died, bequeathing to the Metropolitan plan the success his own had earned, and with it, through his children's love, the lands he had pledged to it.

Mr. De Las Casas takes leave of him with, "His death was thought to have been hastened by overwork in this cause, and to be an irreparable loss to the whole movement." And, as speedily as possible to put his quietus on this popular hallucination, he introduces the Metropolitan share in it thus:—

The agitation became even more energetic, however, when real estate speculators bought the woods along Ravine Road, cut off the grand pines, and turned the scene of beauty into the hideousness of a logging camp. The Appalachian Club took up the matter, and April 2, 1890, appointed Charles

Eliot, George C. Mann, and Rosewell B. Lawrence to arrange for a meeting of all persons interested in the preservation of scenery and historical sites in Massachusetts.

And this meeting, according to his account, by a sequence of other efforts and events was what resulted in the Metropolitan Park law of 1893. The Ravine Woods destruction took place, you will remember, in 1881; and, as we have seen, the "increased agitation" consequent upon it was solely due to the increase of Mr. Wright's own effort in the passage of his law and in every other direction, and, if any part of the Appalachian motive, or that of the other powers concerned, was to prevent further such mischief in the Fells or elsewhere, and Mr. Wright's plan was deemed impractical, to have waited from 1881 to 1890 before appointing that meeting in behalf of something not so hardly seems one of the practical necessities of a more practical method. Nor does it show on their part any very alarming amount of energy. Mr. Wright was a member of the Appalachian Club; and at the time of the Ravine Woods calamity, if my memory serves me, he escorted the membership through the Fells, and urged activity in its behalf. And in 1884, the year he was trying to get organized help for his own then matured plan,—such as a large and popular club might easily have offered,—he lectured before one of the meetings, and at this meeting his plan was not lacking in warm approval. But, if the membership still thought it impracticable, why not have told him that they were going to appoint a meeting April 2, 1890, at which a more practical plan would be discussed, one not only securing his Fells, but his Blue Hills? It was then only seven years before this meeting, and they would not only have had *his* warm approval, but his heartiest co-operation. But maybe it was their wish that he should have no share in the Park success or consummation, should it be gained through their means.

Mr. De Las Casas's little effort at diplomacy is not the only source warranting the inference. Mr. Wright possessed that adjunct of creative power,—enthusiasm. Mr. De Las Casas mentions the trait, both in him and in others most in earnest for his plan, as a failing naturally productive of the impractical. And Rosewell B. Lawrence, secretary of the Appalachian Club, publishes the following from the pen of Mr. T. W. Higginson in his pamphlet, "The Middlesex Fells," of 1886, which was delivered before the club after Mr. Wright's death:—

We miss from among us the face of that devoted friend of all out-door exploration,—Elizur Wright. I have known him almost all my life: first as the fearless ally, and at times the equally fearless critic of William Lloyd Garrison; then as the translator of La Fontaine's Fables,—a task for which he seemed fitted by something French in his temperament, a certain mixture of fire and *bonhomie* which lasted to the end of his days; then as a zealous petitioner before the legislature to remove the lingering disabilities of atheists; and then as the eager, hopeful, patient, and unconquerable advocate of the scheme for setting apart the Middlesex Fells as a forest park. I served with him for a time on a committee for that seemingly hopeless object, and shall never forget the inexhaustible faith with which he urged it. In his presence it was almost impossible not to believe in its speedy success. All obstacles seemed little before his sanguine confidence, and each scattering donation of a dollar or two filled him with renewed faith, although it was plain that tens of thousands of dollars must be forthcoming to accomplish the end. Scarcely any one was ever present at these committee meetings except the three old men in whom the whole enterprise seemed to centre,—Wilson Flagg, John Owen, and Elizur Wright. They were all of patriarchal aspect. As they sat leaning toward each other with long gray locks flowing, I always felt as if I was admitted to some weird council of old Greek wood gods, displaced and belated, not yet quite convinced that Pan was dead, and planning together to save the last remnant of the forest they loved.

Mr. Lawrence calls this an "appropriate eulogy," and Mr. Higginson says he has known Mr. Wright almost all his life.

I have known him *all* mine,—known him in the sunshine of his happy nature's own creating and in the times when, sore with the injustices heaped upon him, it was not easy to creep from the wreck they had made of his plans or to nurse to life the hope they had bruised, but for humanity's sake, and knowing its necessity, he did it. And it is not true that "all obstacles seemed little before his sanguine confidence," or that "every scattering donation of a dollar filled him with renewed faith," or that he was ignorant of the amount of money necessary. Mr. Higginson paints a better picture than he does portrait; for his imagery, with all its rhetorical force, pathos, and vividness, leaves the false but, to the later projectors, the desirable impression that enthusiasm—that wine of the soul—was not only *all* that sustained Mr. Wright during those long years of courageous persistence, but that it *turned his head* as to what was self-evidently impracticable. Mr. Higginson, after acknowledging the *contagion* of Mr. Wright's enthusiasm, might at least have recognized its worth as a *stimulant* to the exertion necessary to success; for, though not potent enough to draw the coy dollars from private purses, it *did*, as it turned out, create the enterprise by which they were later drawn from the public purse. That Mr. Wright possessed, and encouraged in himself and others, enthusiasm, is not to be denied, but that it operated at the cost of his reasoning powers is wholly false. From the day he took up his pen in the cause of the slave till the day he laid it down in that of the Fells, there is hardly a problem affecting the welfare of humanity that he has not dealt with in all its complex and multitudinous bearings; and I could quote here many passages which, in the light of to-day's events, read as a prophecy. Has not the power to generalize, which made him one of the acknowledged first mathematicians of America and, applied to life insurance produced, in its truth to its avowed purpose and to some extent the morality of its management, practically a revolution in its time, something to say for the solidity of his powers and his practical sense? Are not these "Appeals" some little proof that he thought as well as felt? When a short time before his death, after hope for his own plan had been long cheated on empty diplomatic promises, he said, "It is bound to succeed," not enthusiasm spoke, but insight into cause and effect. And did not the later movers themselves, whatever any one of them may say, *practically* prove it when they baked their park pie over the fire he had built for it? And, although in keeping to their corner till he had no longer breath to fan its flames, they played "Jack Horner" to his happiness in the success, had their plum been pulled out and "What a big boy am I!" cried, not at the expense of his share in it or the truth, the filial porcupine within me would never have raised a defensive quill.

But when I see their machinery, as in the infestation matter it now is, getting the better of their success in a way to depreciate, if not ultimately to defeat, not only Mr. Wright's more comprehensive purposes, but, "as advertised" in the "preservation of scenery," their own, my right to protest is another matter. And, having appealed to the proper authorities in vain, what I have to say shall be recorded here. I know that in so doing I play the small dog who barks at the locomotive, and whose warning, if it is not drowned in its noise, is pretty sure to be turned to his own harm, or, worse, to that of the endangered lives he would save; but his dog's instinct of danger ahead is sharp, and, where his sense of right and his love are involved, hard to suppress, and, if the engineers will not heed him, it is not his fault. He has done his best for the precious freight.

The infestation is a frightful calamity; and nothing is of greater importance than that it should be kept under and, if possible, cured, especially in our Fells. But it was proved by the frantic chopping and burning of the Moth Commission that fire and axe as a remedy, while promising, in its results no *greater* ultimate success than with a greater patience can be achieved without them, only increases the destructive mischief or adds to it, leaving in the spots of its trail not only a present charred and blackened desolation quite as disheartening, but for some time a "logging-camp hideousness" especially its own; and its adoption by the Park Commission is to me stronger evidence that the favor of the earlier Commission and its host of short-sighted and careless supporters is politically, perhaps financially, desirable than of any great practical sense on its own part. Certainly, the "views" left after weeks and weeks of chopping and hacking in the little valley of Brown's Brook—a part of Mr. Wright's old home grounds—last fall, and the chopping and burning on and about his Pine Hill this spring, are far more the views of the Moth Commission than of anything with a single thought of the "preservation of scenery."

The lovely woods passing Mr. Wright's grounds and my home were also denuded of many of its larger and finer trees, and it was to save what remained of it below me that I made my appeal. Time to act by letter being too short, I began it by proxy; and the promise of a hearing both on the roadside woods and on our anti-fire and axe views from Commissioner D. N. Skillings, of Winchester, was obtained. It was not kept in either case; and in a letter which would have me believe the tree destruction necessary against the infestation, which through his Board's Secretary he substituted, Mr. Skillings says that "the fight against the gypsy moth" has been left largely by his brother commissioners to him, and that "the work done in my neighborhood was by his direction, and that he assumes the responsibility therefor." Consoling to the tree-destroying consciences of the others concerned, but I fail to see what comfort he expected it to be to me or what help to my cause. Having by an experience covering the infestation up to the present year 1904, in some thirty or more acres of woods as liable to be stripped as any in our neighborhood (more so than most places where fire and axe have been the resort), seen the pest successfully kept under without tree destruction, I am convinced that what is needed is a law prohibiting fire and axe except in the care of the dead and against wild brier, thus preventing the waste of time and labor which ought to be spent on effective means, and under it a body of well-instructed men, in number suited to the exigency, whose duty shall be annually to search for and, wheresoever they may be found, to paint eggs; and especially vigilant should the search be during the fall months, before the low eggs are disturbed or the snow sets in, and among rocks, stones, and stone fences. Throughout the woods of Massachusetts, as in the Fells, there are huge detached rocks, hundreds together, with trees sprung in their cracks, on and under which and the shelving ledges of which the miller hides her eggs; and these hiding-places are, as it were, ovens which, unless a torch were held to each, cannot be heated by fire, for no burning over the ground, use what oil you may, can reach them. But there is not one (and I speak from a good share of personal experience in the search) that cannot be more or less easily reached by the brush. The miller rarely, if ever, seeks shelter too deep or dark to be seen or, if under stones, found. The truth of this —other cleaning being equal—lies in the fact of next year's freedom or marked improvement from the pest. Nor, as I have repeatedly noticed, does it seek stones and rocks at any great distance from badly infested foliage. I am, therefore, confident that, were this SEARCHING AND EGG-PAINTING FAITH-FULLY, THOROUGHLY, PATIENTLY, AND PERSISTENTLY PURSUED FOR THE NEXT FIVE OR SIX YEARS, PERHAPS LESS, we should find the infestation as near "extermination" as, short of including our entire vegetation, it is possible for *man* to bring it; that is, unless the "Pied Piper of Hamelin" happens along. At any rate, we should have got it under a sufficient subjugation to insure the future annual egg-painting against further complete stripping. And it may be the caterpillar-killing could then be left wholly to the birds. We here have seen eating the caterpillars the catbird, wood thrush, oriole, blackbird, cuckoo, and the sparrows, English and American. The greater devastation of this summer, in some measure the consequence of natural causes, is in my estimation infinitely more largely due to the fact that this *most* important and effective part of pest suppression has been, both under public and private management, the one *least* attended to. While in the intrusive caterpillar season spread-checking devices and various means of slaughter have, to some extent, been the regular programme,—and, till the pest is well under, I think should be still,—it has been with the egg-painting, especially in the woods, too much "out of sight, out of mind." And this, too, when EVERY DOLLAR SPENT AGAINST THE EGGS IS WORTH NO END OF DOLLARS SPENT IN ANY OTHER REMEDY OR IN ANY OTHER WAY. Had this not been the case in our neighborhood, our woods, two in number, differently located, and the interiors of which we had, since the abolition of the Moth Commission, all but wholly freed from the pest, would still, as on previous years, not perceptibly have suffered. And that last summer's loss of foliage was still largely in their borders is no unfair support to my position. Being green after their boundary woods were bare, it was their misfortune to receive the migration. And it was the same with my own annually well-cared for grounds; for until "left largely to Mr. Skillings" the "fight against the gypsy moth" on that part of our old Pine Hill directly above them and connecting with the "fire and axe extermination" of its north-east slope had, alike as to eggs and caterpillars, been left so very long a time to nobody in particular that the egg accumulation there, notwithstanding this spring's cutting and burning, was this year such as to set at its own small worth an inadequate eleventh-hour effort of the previous one, and it was thus this summer speedily stripped. And, as during the remainder of the crawling season nothing was done to check the spread or lessen the caterpillars, my grounds were soon completely infested, and would have been as completely stripped, had I not hastened to ink-band certain trees and daily destroy the caterpillar blankets encircling their trunks and, for a yard round, the grass below.

As to the cost of what I propose, since our State is part of a great money "power" which, when the "fight" is to plunder the financial "resources" and subjugate the people of a weaker nation, can equip thousands of men and pay out millions of dollars, of course it need not be counted. Nor, with the demand so imperative, would it be right to do so.

In a park, no matter what it is done for, tree destruction is demoralizing, and therefore dangerous. It tempts a management whose tree-cutting powers are not defined, and who are at the same time politicians, to take out both in quality and quantity what ought to be left; and it sets private owners and land speculators to chopping also, and by cheapening in the popular mind the worth of living trees and their value to human life destroys the public favor on which the perpetuity of the park depends,—a fact which men with other axes than steel ones to grind will not be slow to take advantage of. In support of a course so promising to his building interest the man of the amendment, for instance, has done a deal of chopping in his own infested woods,—I mean those in the Fells neighborhood and ours. Those of his own home, or private park, if infested, I judge, receive a different treatment. Indeed, with much more of this crazy tree destruction, not only on the infestation pretext, but on various other theories and for political reasons, the ultimate fate of our poor little Fells reservation may prove that of the mother who, to appease the wolves by which her sleigh was pursued, threw out first one little child and then another but to be overtaken at last and herself devoured.

Awhile ago permission was asked by the Park Commission of the contributors to the care of the Virginia Woods, now part of the Fells reservation, to use what remained of their money for "general purposes"; and it may be in the price of cord wood not its avowed *special* purpose, but these "general purposes," are to be served by the chopping. In our neighborhood, judging by the wood-piles and cartloads, the trees felled are well calculated to fetch their price as cord wood both in quantity and quality, while among those left standing the respect due the dead and the tenderness due the sickly has not failed of regard. Or, judging by the official responses to my appeals, the service, as I have hinted, may be diplomatic.* Before Medford was dubbed a city, and while yet the Metropolitan Park law was under legislative discussion, I myself received a hint of this possibility in the following little occurrence. I was one day waited on by a down-town gentleman with the request that our Pine Hill should be given to the prospective city. Having some reason to believe that the prospective city was largely the scheme of the man of the building interest amendment, I asked if he had any share in the request. My answer, given with more of caution than of clearness, was that "he was interested in the matter." I told my gentleman then that our Pine Hill was to be given to the Metropolitan enterprise, as the park our father worked for was a State Park, not a local one. And to this he assured me, with some emphasis, that to give it to the city was just the same as to give it to the State or the metropolis an assertion which later found corroboration from the lips, of the town officer behind the little window of the Town Hall, where I had an errand, and who also seemed "interested in the matter." But although not otherwise clear what claim a prospective city which had done nothing for us or our prospective park, except at this very time of its probable success raise the taxes of both by a mighty sudden and high jump, according to its advocate's appraisal, in the value of Medford land, had upon our Pine Hill or our benevolence, I held to my point. Neither gentleman had told me what our hill was wanted for; but, when I learned from another source that its cherished

---

* If the money goes, not to *Park purposes*, but into the State Treasury, it certainly is.

xlix.

woods were to be hacked into in behalf of that ugly jail of a stand-pipe,—by wiser advice now located elsewhere,—I saw why they had let concealment feed upon the damask of their diplomatic cheek. That amendment to exempt the water lands from the park was also under legislative discussion, or rather was to be winked into the law without it; and it was a very pretty little stroke of diplomatic double-dealing to cheat the park of its hill, and to make us pay for the cheating. But the later park compromises necessitated by the amendment and others enforced in behalf of the city do seem to make the State and city the "same thing." And *The City*, where the lion's share of wealth unites with the foxes of cunning in placing through his proxies the balance of administrative power in the hands of a single man, might as well be the alias of that man's name. At any rate to such a man the very existence of a gifted reformer like Mr. Wright is an offence and a source of jealousy,—a fact which is not without support to my surmise that Mr. Wright's views have been made the price of political favor. Nor does it seem to me utterly foreign, either to human possibilities or human nature, that a very small species of retaliation against his children in their public censure of the fire-and-axe espousers may not have had its own place in this price. What we wrote and said, as the following will show, was not received by the Commission Combination without personal resentment.

The moth men were in the habit of utilizing our out-buildings to put their things away in, and one day, chancing to be near one of my brother's barns as a bundle of uniforms, burlap, etc., were being entered, my ears caught with some force from a little distance these words: "You let that—barn alone." How much my proximity to it may have had to do with the outburst, I leave to the imagination; but it was the first time anything, eggs and caterpillars included, had been expelled from a—building of ours. And, after my last paper in the *Transcript* on the Pine Hill burning (my first was when my sister's woods was burned), I heard that the Park Commission were displeased, but "couldn't say anything." Of course not, with the result of the burning against it; but it, or the diplomatic machinery owning it, could *do* something. And shortly after a later contribution of mine, written by editorial invitation in response to a paper on the other side, had been received at the *Transcript* office, measures were taken by which it did not appear, while certain other contributions indirectly condemning its writer's position were given space. And, if my particular "Mr. Judas" did not make direct appeal against me to the *owners* of the paper, his spirit was certainly "hovering near" *somewhere* among them. And now if, after being *practically* assured by the official tree doctors of the Fells that to go on killing the patients of an epidemic is the way—or any way—to cure the disease, and in solemn *words* that in all their official doings their judgment "is based upon that of expert advisers," I have persisted in looking for other reasons than its own merit, or theirs, to account for what seems to me not only impractical, but, in a park where forestal benefits *ought* to have *no unimportant place among its purposes*, morally wrong, I cannot be blamed. For the very wheels on which their diplomatic machinery is run, even its own workers will proudly acknowledge, is not truth or fair and open dealing, but processes of indirection that are the reverse,—in other words, whatever is expedient, right or wrong; and I cannot therefore against the evidence of my own senses accept any unsupported statements.

My appeal to the Park Commission for the roadside woods was not the only one I had been compelled to make to it. There was an earlier and, antecedent to it, circumstances which should have strengthened my claim to a different treatment than the polite diplomatic bluffing off it received. In my correspondence with the Commission, as well as in deeding my share in the Pine Hill gift, the hope that the trees of our father's former grounds, the trees which he had been at such cost to rescue from the axe, should never be felled by it, had not failed of definite expression. In my deed that they should be preserved in his memory was the motive of my gift; and in retaining a life interest in my home, also a part of my settlement, to live with the assurance that they were now safe was my hope. That the Commission fully understood this, their letters, presently to be given, will vouch. And yet while my gift, so far as I know, was accepted without discussion, consent to my life lease, perhaps in contemplation of later tree-destroying schemes,—*one* certainly,—would not have been granted but that I had an able advocate and a sympathetic friend in Philip A. Chase, then one of the Commission. And just here I shall digress for the pleasure of adding to my record another act of this gentleman's generosity and true sympathy.

It was his proposition to have placed in Mr. Wright's memory, and in honor of his lion's share in the Park cause success, a little stone structure on Pine Hill. Mr. Wright did not let the stones cry out to him in vain for his Fells salvation, and it was not unfitting that they should speak for him in return; but it was not what he would himself have sought. To have fostered his hope of forestal benefits, that the words of his old friend Whittier to another brave worker for Nature and humanity, "Grateful hearts instead of marble shaping his viewless monument," might be true in his case, was the tribute he would best have liked. And it would not have mattered to him, had his share in the *gratitude* been all given to the later movers. Gladly did he while living pluck laurels from his own brow, that they might be placed wherever it seemed best for his cause that they should be. But with me it does matter. And the stone-structure proposition coming from Mr. Chase had worth which none other could have given it; for that *his love of the woods was my father's own* not only has its voucher in the patient and persistent work by which his "Lynn Woods" was saved,—may its trees against the right of

his own memory to regard and honor never be destroyed,—
but in other ways. There was hardly a day, his wife told
me, that he did not visit this woods, and often he was the boy
again for a whole day's ramble. And on one occasion, when
he somewhere chanced to come upon tree butchers in the act
of destroying a fine old woods, to him indeed "God's first
temple" and that of his own worship, he begged suspension
of operations till he could see the owners, and then, not to
lose a second of the brief time granted, ran all the way of
the goodly distance it was his to go. With *such credentials*
to Park guardianship his early withdrawal from the Commission was a public misfortune. And they certainly won both
my favor and my co-operation in his proposition for the stone
structure,—a co-operation by which about ten or eleven hundred dollars were contributed to it, and the vote of the Commission to furnish the rest of the cost—about $2,000, in Mr.
Chase's estimation—and to put it up obtained. Why it has
thus far been also of a "viewless" character is best known
to the present Commission. But, if what I write here is ever
read, "gratitude" to Mr. Chase in the heart of one small person shall not be so.

To return to my appeals. After the Moth Commission
had been for some two years abolished, the axe of the Park
Commission appeared on my share of the Pine Hill gift. It
could hardly have been against the infestation, for at that
time it was confined all but wholly to that exterminated northeast slope. The superintendent of the chopping said it was
done to give the little pines a chance to grow. But as there
were no little pines anywhere near most of the trees cut, and
as the Commission, though appearing now to spare them, had
shown little care for the larger number destroyed by the moth
men, this as a reason seemed also susceptible of doubt. The
chopping had begun out of my sight and hearing, and had
gone on for about a fortnight, I afterward heard, before I
discovered it. And, when I did, it was three or four days

more before I could get hope enough in my success to say a word against it. But, when I did and received the following, I was sorry I had not spoken sooner:—

I regret very much that you should have been annoyed by the tree-cutting on Pine Hill, and have ordered it stopped at once. I will have no further work done there without consultation with you or your brother.
Yours very truly,
JOHN WOODBURY, *Secretary.*

In returning thanks, I told the Commission that, unless it notified me otherwise, I would consider its promise to include my brother's gift also, the Pine Hill woods west of mine, and received the "consent of silence."

Responding to my roadside woods appeal, Secretary Woodbury for Commissioner Skillings further says:—

He was aware of and in sympathy with the feeling of the Commission that nothing should be done on the estate formerly belonging to your family in the removal of trees, *so far as the Commission deem it possible to go in the exercise of their official duty.** He did not, and does not now, understand, however, that this was the position of the commission in regard to the trees and shrubbery in the highways which were formerly in the control of the city of Medford, and have now been turned over to the control of this Commission by the city for care and control. He desires me further to say that he has directed cutting in the neighborhood of your residence to be stopped for the present, and that it will not be resumed until the Commission as a body has an opportunity to pass upon the necessity of the work as planned.

In answer to this I wrote:—

PINE HILL, August 22, 1903.
DAVID N. SKILLINGS AND OTHERS OF THE METROPOLITAN
    PARK COMMISSION:

Gentlemen,—Although I think it would have been fair, in so far as the tree destruction passed my grounds, before pro-

* Italics mine.

ceeding with it to have given me time to see you, by serving the abutter's thirty days' notice as the law demands, my note did not, as the letter by Mr. Woodbury surmises, assume any indebtedness on the part of your Commission to me or mine, "in regard to the trees and shubbery of the highway." My appeal was to your humanity as men having the power at little, if any, cost to their own plans, to save me further pain. And I think your disregard, alike to my right of notice and to the beauty of my own home according to my own taste, entitles me to at least what little reparation would lie in the sparing of what is left of that roadside woods. I will try and hope that your meeting "to pass upon the necessity" of its destruction to your "work as planned" will, in its decision, spare both the trees and me. But far more earnestly and anxiously do I hope that you will not forget the most important necessity of the work as planned by Nature in the pure air to a crowded city which the preservation of woods in her Fells and Blue Hills, the only two spots where anything like a forest is possible, alone can give.

In subjecting to you what I would now say, my petition is still not on any legal claim, for I have none, but upon your sense of justice in what I hold to be right in my particular case. When I expressed the hope in my deed of gift that the living trees on and about Pine Hill should never be felled, I thought your Commission in sympathy with father's objects, if not his plan; and that in your appreciation of their wisdom, and that long and generous labor on his part by which the success of your own plan was made possible, you would hold my hope as an obligation. To me your acceptance of the gift implied that you would. Your cutting on Pine Hill undeceived me. But the promise given in answer to my plea, that no further cutting should be done without consulting us,—by which I had a right to conclude that you held our consent to it necessary,—assured me that during our lives our trees were safe; but from Mr. Woodbury's letter it would seem that they are not,—except subject to what you may consider official duty, —and I am left still in continual dread of the axe. Now, although my settlement with you in relieving me of taxes is financially helpful, for which my thanks, in view of the fact that by some $70,000 salvation on our sales as compared with others on land similarly located, and by our gifts, the financial indebtedness is far larger on the side of the Commonwealth, and in view, also, of the fact that our loss in trees, deemed valuable by us, has in one interest and another already been large, I think it not too much to ask of you a written pledge that no trees on our father's former estate shall hereafter by any act of yours be removed, except the dead and such, and for such reasons as I may, on consultation while living, have approved, but shall forever be preserved in accordance with our wish herein expressed. And, further, that the caterpillar infestation shall be yearly attended to without the use of fire and axe.

If you cannot give me this pledge, it would seem to me fair that you pay me a reasonable sum for my life interest and my share in the Pine Hill gift, that I may have the means of living elsewhere; and, since I cannot honor my father's memory by protecting his trees, may honor it in some other way.

Yours respectfully,

ELLEN M. WRIGHT.

To this I received no *answer*, but the following substitute from Mr. De Las Casas, whose diplomatic effort in this instance to write with "sufficient dubiousness" to at once make me think his Board's regard for my hopes something besides a mere farce, and at the same time to make it plain that, "for all me," it would do as it pleased, is hardly the shining success of the immortal Mark Twain when acting as private secretary to the same machinery.

BOSTON, Sept. 9, 1903.

Miss ELLEN M. WRIGHT,
Forest Street, Medford, Mass.:

Dear Madame,—The Metropolitan Park Commission have received and given careful consideration to your letters of August 13th and August 22d, and desire me in reply to express their deep regret that you should be annoyed by the work which the Commission feels obliged to carry on in the neighborhood of your home for controlling the ravages by the gypsy moth. We appreciate and in general share your deep regret at destruction of trees and shrubbery. We wish to spare your feelings and, as far as possible, to show the appreciation of the community at the liberality of your family. We beg, also, to assure you that we will always listen and give respectful consideration to your wishes and views. In so doing, however, we cannot promise to always agree with you or to reach your conclusions, as our duty requires us to finally reach our own conclusions.

When your family gave land, and when the city of Medford gave streets to the Commonwealth, it was under a law which required members of this Board to take and exercise the care of them; and the present members of the Board are conscientiously acting under this law to the best of their abilities. In the exercise of this duty it is possible that our judgment, based upon that of expert advisers, is not as good as your own, and for that reason, as well as out of consideration for your generosity, we shall not act contrary to your wishes when we can see our way to conform to them. But we must say plainly and firmly that, while we know your general views and will always be glad to know your views as to special matters and, so far as is reasonable, consult you when any act is likely to affect your immediate surroundings, yet when action is taken, whether after consulting you or not, you must assume that it is, except through occasional inadvertencies, final and based upon careful consideration and decision. We sincerely hope that such action will interfere with your views or your comfort as little as possible.

I remain, yours respectfully,

W. B. DE LAS CASAS, *Chairman*.

From the second paragraph of this letter it would seem that a *law*, and not, as stated in Mr. Skillings's letter, a *later transaction*, is to blame not only for the roadside destruction, but for that on the "estate formerly belonging to your family," also. However, I don't doubt the existence of the law. I only think that it must read, "Whereas, if by gift, purchase, or devise any lands or streets shall be ceded to the Commonwealth in behalf of the Metropolitan Park system or any park or parks thereof, said lands or streets having trees and shrubbery upon them infested by insects or liable to insect infestation shall be considered a public nuisance, and it shall be the duty of the commission, board, management, or other legally appointed authority conscientiously acting under this law to the best of their abilities to remove said trees, and it shall be no excuse, let, or hindrance to the execution of this duty that any part of said lands or streets may have been *accepted under opposite conditions*," etc. And, if it does not and still puts no limit to the tree-destroying powers of the Commission, I only think that, since the law was in existence when "my family gave land," its conscience, "acting under it," need not have suffered had it, as a gift, refused that land, or at least been kind enough to have told us of the law, that we might use our own judgment in the matter of the gift.

The Commission, according to Mr. De Las Casas, "appreciates and in general shares our deep regret at the destruction of trees and shrubbery." I don't know whether "in general" means that it doesn't share it where its *own* wishes are concerned or that it doesn't do so where *ours* are. But, if actions speak louder than words, it is the latter and, as Mr. De Las Casas likes what is practical, I would ask him where practically, in general or in particular, was this "appreciation" expressed? Was it when the Commission, knowing its motive, made its first cutting on *my* share of the then not perceptibly infested Pine Hill gift, or when, by a *condition made later for the purpose*, it this spring broke its promise not to do so again without consulting us in favor of an infestation very largely the result of its own neglect? But perhaps it was not *neglect*, but, with the design of furnishing some apparent reason for the same tree destruction on our *former grounds* as elsewhere in the *Fells*, it was a part of "the work as planned."

Remember the Fells generally is not yet much, if at all, infested; and in time to have saved it, or, at least to have prevented the total annual ravage now threatened, to have cared for the hill we *gave* it to care for, would have been both practical and honorable. It is not thus that the Commission has treated "The City." What remains of the street trees it has this spring taken measures to save or keep green. But to kick the ladder by which it has mounted and to kiss the rod by which it has been smitten is a large part of the administrative policy it has adopted as the right machinery. Or was it when, after carting off its good cord wood, the Commission left the unchecked pest to spread not only through the uninfested hill woods, but into my all but uninfested grounds? Was the object here to make it harder for me to hold my home by making me do *its* work? By the practical evidence it would seem so. Or was it last fall when Mr. Skillings, to whom the "fight is largely left," aware of the Commission's "feeling that nothing should be done in the way of removing our former trees, and in sympathy with it," after a delay which played Tantalus to my hope of something better, or at least not worse, not only ordered down the remainder of the roadside woods, but most of the trees and all the wild growth of our once exquisitely picturesque "Brown's Brook" surroundings, and not only that, but went further, that on the border of our old pond a great garden of wild roses and other flowering shrubs might be completely hacked down? These endeared spots were our lifelong pride; and, although at a little distance a few trees were badly infested, the infestation had not yet caught perceptibly into either. And that flowering field had always been encouraged by us as a lovely offset to the now large and vigorous young pines which father and I had planted together on the pond's hither side. But it may be that to destroy uninfested places furnishes a better support to the fire and axe fad than can be obtained of badly infested ones.

Or was it when, in "Uncle Remus" phrase, it "cohorted" with the Metropolitan Water Board, instead of taking its pipes under the street where they belonged and *practically* could have gone, to lay them under my Pine Hill via my sister's lands? That "appreciative" undertaking left a great gap through my sister's woods, rendered her stone quarry lix.

practically valueless, and depreciated her land for building lots; and in my own case, for nearly three months, turned my quiet, clean, private paradise into pandemonium with the deafening noise of steam-engines and drills and into a public dump for filth and clutter. Every one of the large and valuable trees along the pipe line, which the engineering officials—each one of whom separately assured me that *he* was the head of the whole thing, and that what he said was law— had promised me *should* not and *need* not go down, were at different times, when my back was turned, destroyed; and within the three or four acres of the pipe-laying operations hardly a tree that was not barked or in some way mutilated. My grass was ploughed up by the dump-carts, my woodbines torn from the house by the blasting, my fern and flower beds trampled into, and my fruit garden wholly destroyed. And before this *unwarrantable trespass*, so far as my own private park share was concerned, though sometimes visited by park ramblers and always by the neighboring boys in apple and cherry time, I had never once had to cry, "Janet, donkeys!" or rather Janet something worse. And, when it came to reparation, both my sister and myself found the Board as niggardly of its damages in dollars and cents as it had been prodigal in injury. Mine I did not contest. Having learned of a lawyer that under the *law* assault and battery to the senses and the soul, with intent to kill their dearest objects, is *no injury*, and that my claim was good only for actual cost, and of Mr. Dooley that court decisions follow the "electioneering returns" by which the *law*-makers are made, I spared myself the vexation and interminable delay. But having also some little knowledge of my own from the recording books, where it would seem, in the financial sense, that damages are alone for those who, if they don't get what they claim, have financial teeth which, to the cost of the refusal, they can show, I would like to see which of the honorable gentlemen of that Water Board, had his own peace of mind and his own grounds been treated as mine were, would be willing to take as reparation only $350, the settlement sum thought to be *all-sufficient* both in my sister's case and mine. It seems to me that this sort of appreciation, sympathy, and share in our deep regret is altogether too much like a man I once heard saying soothing words to the kittens he was drowning.

And the Commission, through Mr. De Las Casas, would also, "as far as possible, show the appreciation of the community for the liberality of my family." And here I would ask whether it was shown by Mr. De Las Casas himself in his *depreciation* of its head member's memory *to* the community through the *New England Magazine*, or in his Board's failure to put up the more appreciative stone structure on Pine Hill, or in its different efforts there to destroy, in his trees, the memento we ourselves had elected should stand? To have refrained from the magazine depreciation, and, with more than half its cost in the treasury, and the remainder voted for, to have established the stone structure, would, at least, not seem outside the possible. As has been said, the object of my family's liberality was, to the extent of its smaller powers, to *represent* its *head's appreciation* of the blessed fact that his Park cause had at last been consummated by an enterprise which could not but, to a generous degree, be beneficial to the community for which he had striven, in the *practical* way in which he would himself have *represented* it; but not so in regard to *our* liberality, the Commission. Whatever it may have done or been willing to do independently, in the way sought it has been the reverse of practically appreciative. And whether in so being it has represented the community, itself, or the politicians and *The City*, my reader is welcome to decide. It has certainly not done much to make the *right machinery* practical or the "best policy," *honesty*, the accepted one.

Where shall we keep the holiday,
And duly greet the entering May?
Too strait and low our cottage doors,
And all unmeet our carpet floors :
Nor spacious court, nor monarch's hall,
Suffice to hold the festival.
Up and away! where haughty woods
Front the liberated floods;
We will climb the broad-backed hills,
Hear the uproar of their joy;
We will mark the leaps and gleams
Of the new delivered streams,
And the murmuring rivers of sap
Mount in the pipes of the trees,
Giddy with day, to the topmost spire,
Which for a spike of tender green
Bartered its powdery cap;
And the colors of joy in the bird,
And the love in its carol heard,
Frog and lizard in holiday coats,
And turtle brave in his golden spots;
We will hear the tiny roar
Of the insects evermore,
While cheerful cries of crag and plain
Reply to the thunder of river and main.
Ralph Waldo Emerson.

MOUNT ANDREW PARK.

[Nov. 5, 1869.]

The question of a proper City Park cannot be properly or finally settled without very liberal views of space and time.

What is wanted is not a local breathing-hole, like our Common, that would be crowded if more than the neighboring population should meet there. Of such we have some — and should have many more — oases in the great desert of populous brick and mortar.

Steam has accomplished, or stands ready to accomplish, this miracle for future ages, that a City Park which is wholly outside of the city, free from its noise and from the dust and smoke of its traffic, will be effectively more accessible to its population than if it were central. Given a steam railroad whose terminus is the centre of a great city, and whose rates of fare are controlled by the city itself, it is plain that the *use* of a sufficiently large City Park — to say nothing of its creation — will cost the city less than if the same space were perfectly central, obstructing the immense internal traffic that must go around, or through, or under it.

What is the Boston that wants a City Park?

It is not any one particular municipality of the four or five that occupy the remarkable cluster or convention of peninsulas in this neighborhood. It is the whole aggregation or community of commercial and manufacturing population, which is rather bound together than separated by the fast-narrowing watercourses that have hitherto served as political boundaries. A cat may have a persistent horror of crossing a watercourse. But a great city cannot afford to indulge such a prejudice, whether, in crossing, it annexes itself to a smaller city or a larger. The interests of all honest citizens, whatever the width of the ditches between them, are common; and, provided the said ditches are no obstructions to the progress or circulation of dishonest people, there should be a common government. Hence, in the end, there will be.

If Boston makes a park that will only do for the present municipality of that name, a larger Boston will soon have to make another. By suiting herself as she will be, perhaps she will do the very best to suit herself as she is.

The most desirable qualities of a City Park may be stated as follows : —

1. It should have a large extent,— not less, certainly, than 2,000 acres.

2. It should be surrounded by a nearly equal territory, so under control of the city that it can exclude from it all nuisances, and keep it devoted to tasteful and cleanly residences and occupations.

3. Its site should be high and perfectly drainable, affording the greatest variety of surface, and eminences overlooking the whole city, the sea, and the interior of the country.

4. It should be well wooded and well watered, having the finest lake scenery, natural or artificial.

5. It should be capable of being made a museum for the study of every branch of natural history, as well as an attractive retreat into the domain of wild nature herself. It should not only have luxuriant gardens, groves, and forests, but rocks that are both instructive and sublime.

The Boston public generally is quite unaware that nature has provided and held in trust for Boston a site exceeding 4,000 acres in extent, all within eight and one-half miles of its city hall, on which all these qualities may be realized at a moderate expense.

This territory was first explored two hundred and thirty-eight years ago by its discoverer, Gov. John Winthrop; and this is his account of it, extracted from his diary : —

February 7, 1631. (O. S.) The governour, Mr. Nowell, Mr. Eliot, and others, went over Mistick River at Medford, and going N. and by E.

among the rocks about two or three miles, they came to a very great pond, having in the midst an island of about one acre, and very thick with trees of pine and beech; and the pond had divers small rocks standing up here and there in it, which they thereupon called Spot Pond. They went all about it upon the ice. From thence (toward the N. W. about half a mile) they came to the top of a very high rock, beneath which (towards the N.) lies a goodly plain, part open land and part woody, from whence there is a fair prospect; but it being then close and rainy, they could see but a small distance. This place they called Cheese Rock, because, when they went to eat something, they had only cheese, (the governour's man forgetting, for haste, to put up some bread.)—*Winthrop's New England*, vol. i. page 6.

To show how little is known of this beautiful region, it may be stated that Mr. Savage, in editing Winthrop's Diary, in 1825, suggested in a note *birch* instead of *beech*, as the wood that grew on the island. Any one who now visits it will find the wood upon it chiefly *beech*, pine, hemlock, and maple; and it must have been so in the time of Savage. This wood owes its exemption from the furnace to the protection of the surrounding water, for the gem of an island, though a perfect emerald in summer and amethyst in autumn, is so little valued as a thing of beauty, that it was sold under the hammer a year ago for fifty dollars. That is probably fully up to the average price at which the whole 4,000 acres could be bought, and the buildings upon it would be dear at $60,000.

It may be safely asserted that no citizen of Boston, or even South Boston, could to-day stand on "Cheese Rock," with eyes in his head and taste in his heart, even though it should be "close and rainy," and afterwards think of any other site for a City Park.

"A thing of beauty is a joy forever."

Here are more than six square miles of beauty, in spite of the worst the ruthless wood-choppers have been able to do. All that art has to do is to give us easy access to all parts of it without spoiling the beauty.

This will not be the work of a day. All the better for that. A generation or two may well pass in making such a place

what it should be. But a railroad, which should be the first
thing after securing the site and settling the general plan,
may be built in a year, and from the moment of its comple-
tion the Park will be more enjoyable to the mass of our population than anything of the sort that exists on this continent.

But the cost?

That is not a material question. The true question is,—
Will it pay?

Let us see. Suppose ten miles or so of double track rail-
way should branch off from the Boston & Maine, a little
beyond the present Medford branch, leading up one of the
valleys to Spot Pond, crossing over the eastern edge of that
beautiful water on a viaduct, which will cost a million of dollars or two; then traversing the beautiful plain at the north
end of it, and, curving around Gov. Winthrop's "Cheese
Rock," should come along down by Meeting-house Brook
and the Mystic, till it joins and adds another track to the
present Medford branch. Let us suppose the road, including the viaduct, costs \$3,000,000 ready to run thirty trains of
ten cars each around this loop every day. It will certainly
cost to run these trains, as any railroad man knows, keep the
road good, pay the Boston & Maine fairly for the use of its
main track and depot, and pay 7 per cent. on the capital, not
more than \$1,500 per day. Fifteen thousand passengers at
ten cents apiece raises this amount, and they could all be
seated in the trains with 7 or 8 per cent. of the room to
spare. This is only about three-quarters of the visitors that
daily flock to the Central Park of New York, on the average,
at probably a greater average cost. But let us suppose only
one-third of this influx, or 5,000 per day, how long should
we have to wait for the other 10,000?

Let us suppose that the 4,000 acres cost the city twice its
present value, or \$520,000, and this price is assessed on
two thousand acres, to be devoted to building lots. This
would make the building lots stand the city in a little less
than six mills the square foot. Is it objected that the city
would have only 87,120,000 square feet of rocks to sell? Let

it be so. Here are the bones of a paradise, and the flesh to clothe them is only two or three miles this side. We have seen in our own day, a large territory of mud covered with gravel brought nine miles from Newton by steam at fifty cents a cubic yard. Suppose that was the right thing to do, it does not follow that the reverse process of carrying the mud of Mystic flats to cover the hills of Medford and Stoneham, is the wrong one, and especially if by doing it the great want of the three great northern railroad lines, more wharfage, can be supplied. Mud and clay enough to cover four thousand acres two feet deep can be spared from the valley of the Mystic, and the water left in its place will be worth more than the meadows and oyster-beds destroyed. Suppose it costs twice as much to carry a cubic yard of mud up four miles as to bring a cubic yard of gravel down nine miles, then it will cost seven cents and four mills to put two cubic feet of fertile soil on a square foot of rock. This makes the square foot of building land stand the city in eight cents. With two cents more for access to it, the minimum price might be fixed at ten cents per foot including half the adjoining streets, and the whole 87,120,000 would be bid off and built upon, as fast as it could be brought into the market. If occupied in lots averaging a quarter of an acre apiece, it would accommodate a population of about fifty thousand people, and give about ten thousand daily passengers to the railroad. It will be noticed that this operation gives the city two thousand acres for Mount Andrew Park for nothing.

The name is here anticipated. The best beloved Governor of Massachusetts has a right to give his name to the loveliest eminence in what will be a Massachusetts as well as a Boston Park, and that beautiful mount may well name the whole. Spot Pond, which has long refused to answer to the name of Lake Wyoming — a sheer plagiarism — will perhaps consent to be called Lake Winthrop, in honor of its brave and noble discoverer.

To return from the name to the nominee, it may be considered to be abundantly demonstrated that population within half an hour of a great city is governed by the cheapness of transportation. A far lower rate of fare between a man's home and his shop will create a far better paying business than the present. This is a solemn fact which railroad directors in this neighborhood still have the stupidity to ignore or deny to the great detriment, both of their stockholders and the public. Let them not suppose they have a monopoly of the great inventions of Watt and Stephenson. The wit of the dead belongs to all the living. The people have a right, as against either paid-up stock or watered stock, to breathe pure air and see pleasant sights and use the eternal forces of nature to that end, at fair cost. It will be their own fault if through their own proper organization they do not secure the enjoyment of this right. Mount Andrew Park will pay. It may take a keen-sighted corporation to see it at first. But it only waits for the waking up of the people to their own rights and interests to make it their own common property, both the Park and the cheap road to it.

The buggies and coaches object to this Park that they cannot get to it by land. This is a misfortune to them, but not much of one to the *infantry* and foot soldiers, who are likely to be a vast majority, on all sides of the water, as long as it is possible to raise steam. The same wise objection lies against Boston itself to all the cities north of the Charles or Mystic; nevertheless, wheels do not entirely avoid bridges.

This honorable committee will make short work with this or any other objection, should they before making their report stand on a fair day where Governor Winthrop dined on cheese. The surrounding scenery will speak for itself if they will give it the opportunity. In that case, if they are at all inclined to the phraseology prevalent in Governor Winthrop's day, they will report that this vast tract has been preserved a wilderness through more than two centuries, down to this age of overcrowded population and steam by a remarkable interposition of Divine Providence. And such a wilderness it is, they will find, if they explore it, that the same thing might happen to-night which happened to the excellent governor soon after he discovered it, who going out to shoot got lost in the woods and took shelter from the rain during the night in an Indian's hut which he found vacant. But before morning a lady, whom he calls a "squaw," came seeking the same shelter and he was obliged to bar her out.

THE PARK QUESTION.

[*Boston Daily Advertiser*, April 26, 1871.]

The well-guarded park bill of last year, which submitted the whole problem of the future beauty and grandeur of our city to a competent and impartial commission, was defeated in the interest of projectors who have manifest private ends to serve. Everybody has private ends; and the public is not about to forego its own ends lest somebody should be privately benefited by it. It ought to, and it will, do the best it can for its whole self, without injury to any individual, and if any individual is enriched by it, so much the better for her or him.

Let us have fair play and no dog-in-the-manger.

Look at Boston. It is highly aquatic,— a good place to come to in ships. It was built in a highly higgledy-piggledy style, in the days when land locomotion was slow and small. You came in a ship and you went away in a ship. The ocean is not abolished, but is as extensive as ever, and none the worse for steam. Stick a pin here. Let us keep all our oceanic facilities undiminished, so that if trade ever *should* be free, or good General Grant get the rest of the world annexed, ships may come into the very most intimate of our alimentary canals.

Maritime Boston, in these last days — though some of our park projectors do not seem to have found it out — has had added to it almost infinite facility of land locomotion. It is almost as if we might all have practical wings grow on our shoulders at will. Men and things come to us from all corners of the continent on iron, so that Boston is almost as ferruginous as it is aquatic. In fact, the iron and the water come to us so nearly on the same level that they rather interfere with one another. The iron is crowding too much on the water; and the ships complain that, whereas they by their very nature are restrained to whatever level the tides please, the iron road is free to choose any level, *ab inferis usque ad cælum*, and yet it has got right in their way, and established a "draw" which is a nuisance to both parties; and, what is worse, in coming from the land it brings a great deal of land along, and dumps it into the water, so that the latter, in spite of its ancient title and its tidal protest, is crowded out. This is not the generous thing, nor the fair thing, nor the wise thing.

If the iron roads don't want to stilt themselves up in the air so as to let the ships sail under, they can burrow beneath the water, and come into the heart of the city that way. The train need not then pitch into an open "draw" or wait for a vessel that is too big to get through. Major-General Foster, a United States engineer, has told us that a tunnel to East Boston will be cheaper than a ferry by $225,000 per annum. Its first cost will be between two and three millions. Any one, by looking on the map, can see how many such tunnels would have to be placed end to end to reach from the Boston & Albany depot to the new town of Everett, going under the Charles and Mystic. The land damages, on a level below the ships, will not be much; and, when the iron roads have made their subaqueous and subterranean accesses and stations and their compound lowering and elevating apparatus for passengers and goods, their present premises above ground will sell for something.

All the clay which composes our nice little peninsula, as well as the sand which chokes our broad estuaries, has been brought down by the rains and deluges of ages from the hills, which it has left sterile and almost treeless. The iron horse can do nothing better than to carry some of it back to the hills, where it is needed.

So we see that Boston is the place where two grand systems of locomotion meet. There is a temporary interference, almost a snarl. The new one has made a sort of invasion upon the old one, and done some inconsiderate, if not foolish, things. This will naturally and necessarily adjust itself in time. We shall see the iron horses, by and by, switching themselves off to their stables in the rural circumference, and the laden trains coming into town of their own accord on a lower stratum, from which ladies and gentlemen will be raised to daylight in the heart of the city, partly by the weight of others going down and partly by steam acting as a balance of power.

In the days of this *e pluribus unum* arrangement, it will be quite easy to have parks, and to get into them, where the air is pure and the vision unobstructed by anything unpleasant.

For example, there is the chain of Blue Hills, overlooking Neponset, Ponkapoag, and the Atlantic. Some of the superfluous clay and mud can go there and make a paradise, after the rattlesnakes are well pickled by the Natural History Society. It will cost but an hour and a dime to go there and back. That grand spot, with which probably few citizens of Boston have anything but a distant acquaintance, is aching to be seized by the right of eminent domain. One only needs plant his feet on its summit in the daytime and open his eyes to see that it is one of the great parks of the future. And this he will as surely see if he climbs Mount Andrew, and, putting his feet on the rock where Governor Winthrop dined on cheese, looks down on the beautiful lake which should have been named after him, but now hides all the loveliness of Scotland under the name of Spot Pond. Here is a park of almost unlimited extent and infinite capabilities, which the owners of the territory would probably be glad to give to the city, and which Chicago, if she could have it at the same distance from her city hall, would give several millions for, *just as it is*. The projectors of the Dorchester Park or of the straggling concatenation of little parklets leading from the Back Bay out to the Chestnut Hill reservoir had better not visit Mount Andrew, especially one of these mornings when the birds are singing, lest their hearts should fail them. Bostonians who know what they suffer from the small and narrow calculations of the past should not be little or mean toward the future, and not drive down stakes in this park business till they have seen for themselves what can be seen from every hilltop within ten miles of the City Hall.

THE PARK OF THE FUTURE.

[*Boston Transcript*, Sept. 25, 1877.]

Nature will have her way at last. Whoever visits Boston one hundred years hence will probably either find not much of a city or will find an immense one, with its principal public park on a site not much thought of now, but which Nature had predestined for it. That site was prepared millions of years ago by volcanic fires bursting up through the slate-rock pavement of an old ocean, and spoiling the surface for any other use to the extent of three or four thousand acres.

The tract was left in the shape of a nearly circular basin rimmed with hills, which here and there rise fifty feet above the top of Bunker Hill monument. Only two or three valleys break their continuity. The interior of the basin is so rugged that our rugged ancestors, after checkering it all over with their characteristic stone fences, and planting apple-trees which seemed to find soil where little is visible to the naked eye, gave it up in despair, and let Nature resume her work of covering and beautifying her own bones in her own way. Now you find the old apple-trees, or their descendants, struggling for breath in groves and forests where Doré would revel. Or, at any rate, you would have done so before the war raised the price of cord-wood. Art could then hardly have improved the forestry of this basin for a park, as Mr. Olmsted, the creator of the New York Central Park, then declared. But the act of converting trees into fuel has done much to mar it. This mischief is, however, by no means irreparable; and Nature is constantly at work to shame, rebuke, and undo the mischief. The site I am speaking of is surrounded by the towns of Malden, Medford, Winchester, Stoneham, and Melrose. The denizens of Summer Street, if any are left, will remember William Foster, who had his summer residence in this very basin, on the eastern shore of what he loved to call Lake Wyoming (vulgarly, "Spot Pond"), and how enthusiastic he was about the beauty of its scenery,— and he had seen whatever is most beautiful in Europe. He had a notion of filling the whole basin with *châteaux*, after the French style; but at last he gave it up, and said — for he was a dreadful democrat — he found "the aristocracy of Boston too stupid to see anything beautiful in nature."

The entire tract is forever proof against any land speculation, for streets in it cannot run at right angles or any angles. Nothing but beauty, in all sorts of curves, is predestined there. Division and subdivision are laughed to scorn. The fantastic, rock-ribbed basin is decreed by the nature of things to remain as a whole — a sort of oasis in a desert of vulgar cultivation — till art condescends to become a handmaid of Nature, and decorate it for the enjoyment and instruction of the whole people. In the sense of its impracticability for ordinary individual purposes, it reminds one of Robert Bloomfield's "skim-milk cheese," of the fate of which he says: —

> "Or in the hog-trough rests, in perfect spite,
> Too big to swallow and too hard to bite."

Now, I am not going to counsel my fellow-citizens of

Boston to buy this for a park, whether by paying cash down or running in debt. Too much of that sort of thing has been done already. The greater part of this land has been devoted to wood lots. But, happily, the roads leading to these lots are so rugged that, unless wood is uncommonly dear, it costs more than it is worth to haul it. Consequently, many lots have been sold for taxes. The land cannot be said to have any market value at all beyond that of the standing fuel. What I propose is that the proprietors of this tract, who mostly reside outside of it and near its borders, shall confer together, and making such an arrangement with each other as to render the sacrifice, if it can be so called, equitable, shall jointly present the whole tract, or all of it with perhaps the exception of three or four elegant little properties, to the city of Boston and the adjacent towns, to be used as a public park, under the control of a board to be properly constituted from the several municipalities, and regulated by a State charter. By this charter the said municipalities should be forever interdicted from spending any money or contracting any debt for the interior improvement of this park, or for anything beyond maintaining order in it; but individual citizens or corporations so inclined should be at liberty, with the consent of the governing board, to make any improvements and erect any buildings for public use and amusement consistent with the general plan devised and published by said board, and to be under the control of the same; and such individuals or corporations should have the credit of such improvements and buildings by record in the books of the park, by names made perpetual, and suitable memorial inscriptions.

In short, instead of driving or frightening away our wealthy citizens by taxing them for future parks, let us have a spot which will tempt them to lay out for the public benefit a good deal of that money which necessarily accumulates in their hands by their being possessed of the capital and machinery which have so much engulfed the little trades.

The arrangement I have spoken of being once made,

private enterprise would soon be making money by carrying people to the park and back for a dime a head. The distance of a park is' no objection, when the cost and time of travel are sufficiently reduced.

Once let the people of Boston see what Nature has done for the site of which I speak, and how enjoyable it is as it is, and the only danger would be that they would be taxing themselves to buy it, and would foolishly deprive the proprietors of the opportunity of doing the wise and politic thing — for I don't pretend it would be generous — of giving it to them. When I speak of giving, I speak as one of the proprietors; for I live on the hither brim of the basin, and I should be glad to make a present of fifty or sixty acres, a tract which for value and beauty of its forest growth, and the grandeur of its outlook, I think is equal to that of any other tract of the same size that would be included in the park. If any of the other proprietors are similarly minded, I shall be glad to hear from them; and my post-office box in Boston is 109. What is perhaps more to the purpose, if any Bostonian, who is not familiar with the site, and wishes to know whether I have overrated it, and is capable of a ramble of four or five miles in pretty rough ways, will give me due notice, I will make myself his guide on any of these fine autumn days, through the blind old cart paths, to the delectable summits, from which he can correctly judge. He will get the worth of his explorative walk in geological and botanical information, if nothing else.

THE RELATIONS OF VEGETABLE AND ANIMAL LIFE.

Next to the sun, moon, and stars, the most wonderful thing we open our eyes upon in coming into this world is the life of which we are a part. As we live and learn, both the lights in the sky and the life we live grow more wonderful. The more the human race learns, the more wonderful they grow. The telescope, invented only two hundred and seventy-three years ago, has magnified the universe to the human mind till the old conception bears to the new less than the ratio of a pinhead to the Rocky Mountains. On the other hand, the microscope has traced life down to living, breeding cells, which no unassisted human eye could ever have discovered. Old philosophers suspected, and now we begin to see, that every atom of matter is alive.

The most wonderful and worshipful thing about life is that duality or distinction of sex which runs from the bottom to the top, from the beginning to the end, from the mass to the man. The next most wonderful thing is the division of it into two almost perfectly distinct departments,— they used to be called "kingdoms," but we had better call them republics,— the *vegetable* and the *animal*, complementary to each other, and almost more necessary to each other than the two sexes. Both, in their hitherto uncounted varieties of organization, on land or in the water, grow by the aggregation and multiplication, under the same general mode or law, of living microscopic cells, from the fungus of a night to the sequoia that towers in the sky for a thousand years, from the wriggling mollusk to the philosopher who measures the interstellar spaces.

Illimitable splendors of light and life, in our day, attract the human mind in every direction. Inexhaustible treasures for study and joy lie on every side. But I propose to limit myself to simply calling your attention, for a few minutes, to the relations of the human being to the tree,— of the human race to the forest,— whether in a hygienic, æsthetic, or economical sense, with a view of converging my remarks upon the practicability and duty of making a public domain of the Middlesex Fells.

"The tree of the field is man's life," wrote the author of the Book of Deuteronomy; and there is nothing truer or more important within the lids of the Bible.

It is a common remark that a man cannot live on air. But he cannot live without it. Nor can any other animal. For, if you exhaust the air out of water, even a fish cannot live in it. Air is also essential to the life of vegetables. The difference, however, between the vegetable and the animal seems to be this: The vegetable eats minerals, whether solid, liquid, or gaseous, even animals if it can get them. It eats air; for its breathing through its leaves is only getting food out of the air, which it is always doing, while it has leaves, in the daytime. But the animal eats no minerals at first hand,— not to grow by, at any rate. It only eats vegetables or other animals. Necessary as air is to it, it eats none. If animals had been placed on this planet before any vegetables, even supposing the air had been fit for them to breathe, they would all have starved to death, in spite of cannibalism. But vegetation, as the rocks, if not the Scriptures, tell us, came first; and to such an enormous extent did it consume its favorite food out of the atmosphere that the air became fit for the breathing purpose of animals, and finally of man. What man or any other animal does in breathing I suppose you all know quite as well as I do, if not better. Nevertheless, I want to dwell upon it a little, because, perhaps, we have not been making the most and the best of what we all know.

The existence of air has probably always been known to mankind. It was one of the four elements of the ancients. But only till lately did any one think it had weight, or know what makes water rise in a suction pump, or run about thirty feet up hill in a syphon. Some said it was nature's horror of a vacuum. But her elements, apparently acting for themselves, without waiting for any word of command, all push, according to their various densities, to get as near as possible to each other, or to some mathematical centre; and infinite space seems to have an infinite number of such centres. Our remote progenitors knew the importance of breathing, and that any animal dies pretty soon after that stops; but they knew so little of the motions of the air that some of them believed the various winds to be a set of inferior deities, who were usually imprisoned in an immense cave belonging to Neptune, the god of the sea, who, when he was good-natured, would let some of them work like ball-and-chain convicts for the benefit of sailors, and, when he got angry, would let out some of the fiercest to strew the shore with wrecks and prostrate the dwellings of men. Bad as is their mischief, it is a very lucky thing for us, breathers, that the winds cut such capers as they do.

For ages men have known a great deal about rocks and metals. The alchemists understood the power of solvents, by which they vainly hoped to transmute the baser metals into gold. But of gases they knew little, of electricity nothing. The word "gas" is not two hundred and fifty years old. It is but little more than a century since no one — not even Solomon — knew that the air we breathe is, at its purest, composed of a mixture of two gases, as different from each other as alcohol and water; viz., one volume of oxygen to four volumes of nitrogen. Most children know that now. But how few, even of adults, realize the vital importance of having this mixture comparatively free from other gases!

The great discovery was made just before our Revolution, by Rev. Joseph Priestley, an English Unitarian minister, and particular friend of Dr. Franklin, who was soon after persecuted for his heresy and republicanism, and driven to this country, where he lived till just six days before the present speaker was born. He may almost be considered the father of modern chemistry; for what could it be without the knowledge of oxygen? As a chemist, he was almost wholly self-educated. Black and Cavendish had discovered a gas which was then called "fixed air" (afterwards carbonic acid) probably a few years earlier. Priestley, however, knew nothing of it till he discovered it himself, and invented "soda water." When a boy, he used to cork up spiders in bottles to see how long they would live without change of air,— a thing not so cruel as corking up children. When he became a preacher, he found time to construct his own chemical apparatus; and, as to the results, I will quote the words of Professor Huxley, delivered at the unveiling of Priestley's statue in Birmingham, eight years ago. Said Huxley on that memorable occasion: "He laid the foundation of gas analysis; he discovered the complementary actions of animal and vegetable life upon the constituents of the atmosphere; and, finally, he crowned his work, this day, one hundred years ago, by the discovery of that 'pure dephlogisticated air' to which the French chemists subsequently gave the name of oxygen."

In regard to human welfare on this planet, these discoveries, particularly that of the "complementary actions of animal and vegetable life upon the constituents of the atmosphere," appear to me to be the most important hitherto to be found in the annals of time. If ever Massachusetts shall have a real forest within a half-hour's ride of its Capitol, the statue of Priestley must be found there.

The school children of this generation probably know — at least, so far as knowledge can be obtained from books — better even than their fathers and mothers that the atmosphere contains, or is liable to contain, in small proportions many other gases besides the vital oxygen and the harmless nitrogen, every one of which is either, like nitrogen, negatively fatal to life when breathed pure, or positively poisonous, and detrimental to health when it makes no more than one per cent. of the air we breathe. That which lies at the foundation of our great question is carbonic acid gas, the choke damp of mines, and the gas that is apt to be fatal to those who descend into wells where a light will not burn till you have thrown down some buckets full of lime-water, and that which causes feeble people to faint in a large audience when doors and windows are closed.

This gas, as we may learn from Webster unabridged, is composed of one part by weight of carbon and two of oxygen. And it is, as modern chemistry has proved, the staple food of the vegetable world.

Carbon is perhaps the most wonderful of all substances. As a pure substance chemists have never caught it, except in a solid state. They begin however to suspect that it is sometimes gaseous. It is crystallized in the most splendid of gems, the diamond, from which it is inferrible that with a high enough degree of heat it would be liquid. But the highest degree of heat artificially applied to carbon, in its common form of coal or lampblack, though it seems to have liquefied or fused it, in exceedingly minute quantities, has not resulted in crystalline diamonds. It is a combustible, and forms the greatest part of the world's store of combustibles, if we exclude the metals, and the hydrogen contained in water, in other words, it is perhaps more than half of the *unburnt* combustible substance of this planet. Perhaps the most wonderful thing about it is its capability of minute division in a solid state. Lampblack is the example, which is obtained from the smoke of a burning lamp. It is the unconsumed carbon which was a chemical constituent of the oil. If the carbon, as well as the hydrogen of the oil, had been consumed, the lamp in a room would be as dangerous as a pan of burning charcoal. But the oxygen of the air coming in contact with the heated hydrocarbon, the oil, greatly prefers the hydrogen to the carbon — that is, it prefers to be producing pure aqueous vapor, rather than noxious carbonic acid gas, or even carbonic oxide gas — which costs it less. So it confines itself to a chemical union with the hydrogen, and allows the carbon to escape in infinitesimal solid atoms wholly unburnt. When the heat of the combustion is feeble these black unburnt atoms are very perceptible as a cloud of smoke, but when by a suitable draft the combustion is made intense, the superheated aqueous vapor, or high steam produced, seems to render them invisible. Perhaps the greater heat splits the visible into invisible atoms. They are not seen as the result of the combustion of kerosene in lamps with proper chimneys, or kerosene stoves for heating rooms. But probably the washerwoman will discover that the linen coming from such rooms has an unusually sombre aspect, and a little microscopic observation would ascertain whether it is the unburnt carbon of the kerosene or not. The solid atoms of carbon floating in the air cannot damage the human lungs like the carbonic acid or carbonic oxide gas, because the passages are so constructed and furnished as to guard against dust, but not gas.

Carbon, as every one knows, makes a large part of every species of wood, and some considerable part of every vegetable and of all the vegetable food consumed by man. Every growing vegetable must procure it, either from the earth, the water, or the air. Chemists and botanists have ascertained that very little of it can come from the soil, either in solid, liquid, or gaseous form, and that plants will grow and build themselves up with carbon in soils and water where no carbon is to be found, also that all which have leaves do absorb carbonic acid gas out of the air, returning the carbon and giving out pure oxygen.

MIDDLESEX FELLS.

O rugged rocks! O hundred hills!
    The handiwork of ancient fires
That laughed to thwart the sturdy wills
    Of our industrious sires!
They walled you into petty lots,
    And sawed your lofty pines,
As if to make a home for goats;
    Or room to dig for mines.
Near by they built a crowded mart
    And left you stark and drear—
You who could shame their highest art,
    And chase the foes they fear.
To build the people homes they stripped
    This city of the trees.
As masts the tallest pines they shipped
    To cross the stormy seas.
Those living steeples in the sky
    We need the air to purify.
O plant the pine! O plant the pine!
    'Tis better than a golden mine.
Its balsam-laden air can heal
    The sorest ills that mortals feel.
Its winter miracle of green
    Upholding spotless white
Should teach our life to be serene
    While shedding purest light.
And when the sun pours fiercely down,
    Your head the pines will cool;
And make it worthy of a crown
    Reflected from the pool.
O plant the pine! O plant the pine!
    'Tis better than a golden mine.

A thousand years may roll away
    And men and maids may come and go,
And yet the pines will not decay,
    But bless the air and all below.

Angelic wings will there abide,
And sanctify the sweetened air,
The thrush will serenade his bride,
And make her nest his sacred care.
Man in his social state doth need
Society of trees,
Or else his burdened lungs must bleed,
Choked by the poisoned breeze.
O when the city's brains are bright,
Its wealth will set this matter right;
A forest then will bless our sight,
In which our poor may draw their breath
Without inhaling seeds of death!

June 10, 1885.

"THE MIDDLESEX FELLS."

[*Massachusetts Ploughman*, Oct. 30, 1880.]

It was a lucky hit of somebody, unknown to me, to attach this title to the extensive region intervening the towns of Malden, Medford, Winchester, Stoneham and Melrose. A fell, says Webster, is the provincial English for a barren or stony hill. In that sense, fells are very common in Massachusetts. Though impervious to the plough, they are nevertheless interesting to the ploughman. They are the source of much of the fertility of our arable valleys. Clothed, in spite of their barrenness, with trees, the rains are always washing down from their tops the elements that enrich our gardens and our corn-fields. Much of this is detained by swamps or floats to the sea. We do not yet make the most of it. We make a still worse mistake if we do not do all that is possible to encourage the growth of trees on all hills that are unfit for the plough. That is cutting off a great source of fertility to the valleys. By denuding the hills of their trees Massachusetts may be turned into a desert. What the human inhabitants of a desert become, we may learn from

Mark Twain and other Eastern travellers. They and their dwellings cut a very sorry figure in the sunlight. The inimitable Mark, distrusting his own reputation for veracity, after describing some of the scenery of Palestine, quotes from William C. Grimes, an authority on the other side, as follows:

" On the northeast shore of the sea was a single tree, and this is the only tree of any size visible from the water of the lake, except a few lonely palms in the city of Tiberias, and by its solitary position attracts more attention than would a forest."

Whenever from Spot Pond, or Cochituate, or Quinsigamond, or any other of our beautiful little Massachusetts "seas," only one tree can be seen, as from the " Sea of Galilee " to-day, our descendants will probably be on a par with the Arabs of Syria, begging for *bucksheesh* of the travellers who visit the ruins of the Hub.

Let one take the road from Malden northward, immediately left or west of the Boston & Maine Railroad, and keeping on up the valley, under the hill, a mile or two, till approaching Melrose, take each turn to the left, he will come out at the seat of Mr. John Botume, on the east shore of Spot Pond. But before reaching it, he will have traversed the Ravine Road, leading through a piece of the finest forest scenery short of California. It would rejoice the heart of Gustave Doré. That is in the Middlesex Fells. And considering the havoc that has been made of trees in other parts of the Fells, it is a miracle of wisdom, reflecting the highest honor on the proprietors that those lofty and valuable trees have not been *felled*.

The Fells are nearly in the form of a square, with the corners a little rounded, and two and a half miles in diameter. They include Spot Pond and Winchester Reservoir, and other possible artificial lakes. Most of the territory is owned in small parcels as wood lots, and a good deal of it is held by tax titles. Much of it is covered with mere brush, which by the carelessness of the owners and of tramps is frequently devastated by fires, and thus prevented from becoming forests. There is no part of it in which the maple, the ash, the walnut, the oak, the pine or the hemlock would not flourish and come to grand perfection, with a trifle of care, saved from the fire and the merciless and mercenary use of the axe.

In an agricultural journal there is no need of dwelling on the immense importance to Massachusetts of timber culture. That has been abundantly set forth. But trees have another, if not a higher value, than that of their timber,— a value in which all have a common interest. They yield while they live an annual crop of health. This is not confined to the individual proprietor. It would be considered, and perhaps would be, tyrannical for the State government, on account of this common hygienic and æsthetic interest of all the people in the forests, to seize those woodlands by the right of eminent domain, and dispossess individual proprietors. But with the consent of individual proprietors, surely the State might accept suitable donations of woodland tracts for scientific, educational and park purposes, and might inaugurate a system for the preservation of the forests, which so far from imposing any additional burden on the tax payers would be the source of some income to the State treasury.

The highest interest of the State is to encourage the spirit of independence and self-support in every individual. This means to encourage practical education, acquaintance with the forces, habits and capabilities of our common mother earth and her multiform children. More and more as civilization advances the happiness of society depends on the general diffusion of knowledge. Science must be popularized or it will prove a curse instead of a blessing. It may be said that a little knowledge is a dangerous thing, but it can be more truly said that science confined to a few enables them to enslave the many. One of the best things ever done by a possessor of wealth for a great city was the establishment of free scientific lectures. If the Middlesex Fells are made a State domain, lectures on the natural sciences will be established there which will be exceedingly attractive to the citizens of Boston and the vicinity. Summer schools of practical gardening will be established, which will tend to make every cottage plat a little Eden of utility as well as pleasure.

If the twentieth century is to be a prosperous one for Massachusetts, a good deal of thinking on the subject of natural education must be done pretty soon.

MIDDLESEX FELLS.

The hilly and rocky tract called the Middlesex Fells was originally covered with a heavy growth of pine and hemlock. In a small part of it oak, maple and ash will grow well and there are beech trees in some spots. There are numerous basins well adapted for the preservation of the natural waterfall if the surrounding hills can be covered with trees and kept clear of human dwellings. This can hardly be done unless the tract is made a public domain and controlled for that purpose. To restore the forests on the hills in any reasonable time, requires the use of all the vegetable mould and muck which will prove a nuisance to the water supply if it remains where it is. The scenery of the Fells is extremely beautiful as it is, and will grow more so as pines are restored to the hills. The forest will pay for its own care and restoration in time; and some revenue may be derived from admitting the public to enjoy the scenery under proper regulations. Less than half a million dollars would put the public in possession of a forest interspersed with natural and artificial lakes of the purest water — a place of resort of inestimable value to a population of half a million people the remotest of whom could visit it in half an hour. The five abutting towns have a common interest in restoring the forest, excluding everything that can contaminate the water and making a public domain which will attract population to its vicinity. Properly cared for and improved this rocky territory would prove better than a gold mine to enhance the value of the real estate in its neighborhood. Divided into small wood lots, it has already been badly spoiled; and if not taken for public use, it will inevitably be still more subdivided and fall into the hands of the least desirable population for dwelling places. Neither the surrounding towns nor our great city can afford this.

"MIDDLESEX FELLS."

[*Boston Herald*, Nov. 1, 1880.]

There have been races and ages in human history in which forests have been treated with great respect. Do the millions of free American citizens know what will happen to their posterity if this regard for forests dies? Do they know that all which is noblest in humanity has grown under great ancestral shades? Do they know that from the shadows of the Caledonian and Hercynian forests have come men of renown, comparable to the sublime oaks that wrestled with the storms of centuries? Do they know that when William the Conqueror, of whom the old chronicles say that "he loved the red deer as if he had been their father," destroyed a multitude of churches and chapels to make room for his fifty or sixty royal forests in England, he committed a wickedness which laid the foundation for the character that exalts the English-speaking people of both continents? England might have been as bare of trees, to-day, as Palestine itself, but for that tyranny of monarchs, which made it as great a crime to fell a tree in one of their forests, as to kill one of their subject men. We, the millions of America, are no longer subjects. Few of us hanker for the royal sport of killing "red deer." Is this a reason why we should treat our glorious forests with ignominious contempt, to be murdered wholesale for the carcass? Of all murders wife-murder is the most horrible. But, in a general sense, animal and vegetable life are a married pair. The forest is the nation's wife. To the husband divorce is death. Will a free nation allow its wife to be murdered by inches? Better send for some William the Conqueror and let him work his will for the sake of shooting deer on our hill-tops and chasing hares and foxes in the glades.

If we are to have millions on millions of healthy, noble-minded men, women and children, we must have our hills crowned with millions on millions of trees and shrubs. The highest wisdom of the nation and state, and especially city, must cherish them almost as if they were human beings.

If science has a voice, let her raise it now, like the trumpets of Doolkarnein, to arrest the neglect and ravage and downright murder of our forests, to arouse the people to fulfil for themselves, in their sovereign capacity, that vital office which selfish kings and luxurious aristocrats have done for the older world of Europe. The way our trees are treated by private ignorance, and our rocky hills robbed of the green robes with which nature strives to hide their nakedness, and to furnish pure air for the lungs of all her living children, pure water for her springs and dewdrops for the grass, is a disgrace to every school and college in our land. The trees surely are as near to us as first cousins. Shall we allow them to be wronged because they are speechless; because they cannot uproot themselves and go about the country as orators; because their ghosts cannot make stump speeches, as men's sometimes do? O, in their pure, secret souls, what follies they accuse us of; what wrongs they treasure up against us!

We have exterminated the axeless savage. Does it follow we must exterminate the forests that sheltered him, and made so much of a man of him as he was? "*Rien de trop*" (Nothing too much), says the old French proverb. We have already transgressed that good rule in our onslaught upon the forests, especially in our Massachusetts hills and rocky intervales, and it is only not quite entirely too late that the Middlesex Fells Association calls on the public to allow a serious experiment to be made, to see if the forests of Massachusetts cannot be better preserved and improved where they are most needed.

THE MIDDLESEX FELLS.

AN ADDRESS DELIVERED AT THE MEETING ON CHEESE ROCK, HELD OCT. 15, 1880.

[*Commonwealth*, Nov. 6, 1880.]

Ladies and Gentlemen: — Assembled on this historic spot, I think you will agree with the poet who said —

"A thing of beauty is a joy forever."

The beauty which you see here is not the work of man or his money, but of nature. She made it, and has preserved it under difficulties; preserved it, I trust, for a larger use to mankind than it has hitherto served.

It is a well-established fact in science that vegetable and animal life are complementary to each other. What is poison to one is food to the other. Were the forests destroyed, mankind would smother in the poison of their own breath. Our health depends, in a great measure, on pure air, and trees are the greatest purifiers, because they absorb the carbon and restore to the air the oxygen essential to the life of animals.

In the neighborhood of great and overcrowded cities, groves and forests become of great sanitary importance. Perhaps no vigorously-growing tree can be destroyed within ten miles of Boston without shortening some human life. At any rate, all the trees within that distance could not be destroyed without making our climate less salubrious than it is, as well as our landscapes more dreary.

Another indisputable fact: The substitution of machinery for handicraft arts has made it absolutely necessary that a far larger proportion of our population should be educated to understand practically the relation of plants to each other, to the elements of air, earth and water, and to the birds, quadrupeds and insects, so that no adult should be found without the art of sustaining life at first hand should the resources of our now minutely divided labor fail him or her. We must teach every child how to raise an ear of corn or a potato, and cook the same, or by-and-bye we may find society burdened with an intolerable amount of pauperism, or what is worse. Education in good citizenship and books is incalculably important, but much of it is, and forever must be, thrown away, or left useless if not applied to things. The best teachers, from Agassiz downward, have discovered that all mankind in our mechanical age need to be kindergartened. That is what the best of them are trying to do.

Now let me state another fact, which I think no man acquainted with the history of property in the vicinity of a great and growing city will dispute. It is that if the wealthy citizens of Medford, Winchester, Stoneham, Melrose and Malden should unite to buy this territory of four thousand acres and present it to the State of Massachusetts, to be used by its people for purposes of education and recreation, every single donor might be richer than before. I believe he would be. It is the great truth conveyed to mankind ages ago in the fable of the "Dog in the Manger." After a man has acquired more than he can use himself the best use he can make of the surplus is to help those who show the greatest desire to help themselves. A great example of this sort here would be catching all over the State.

There are on this territory of about four thousand acres three or four good farms, as farms go in this part of Massachusetts; also, about as many elegant homes for city people as can be counted by the thumb and fingers of one hand. The assessed value of the whole does not probably exceed $200,000. The elegant homes I refer to, on the eastern shore of the lake, are due to the enterprise of Hon. William Foster of Summer Street, Boston, an ardent lover of nature, and whom some people of middle age will remember as the genial friend of their childhood. About the beginning of the century he purchased a considerable tract of land with the intention of founding a suburban city, but with so little success that he finally gave away most of his land to some institution, which allowed it to be sold for taxes. One of his neighbors, the late Mr. Eaton, who owned a charming residence on the lake, offered to give it and a large sum of money besides to the city of Boston if it would adopt this as the site of the great future park. In 1869, when I was a taxpayer in Boston, I advocated the purchase of this tract by the city. But, as I no longer pay taxes in that city, I no longer give that advice. The capitalists of Boston live principally south of the Charles, and in that direction all enterprises for the spread of the city population tend. So far as the action of the city is concerned, this side of the Mystic will, of course, be left out in the cold. But as you see here, with your own eyes, and as some of your ancestors saw two hundred and forty-nine years ago, we on this side of the Mystic have certain natural advantages which, in the long run, will carry the day. We have only to show that we have clear heads and kind, humane hearts.

Now for a practical plan of making a beginning : —

First, we want a plan wide enough to interest everybody and bring everybody face-to-face with nature herself. Let there be an association to obtain this. Let it ascertain from the tax-lists the assessed value of all the property embraced in the described territory. Let it then circulate a subscription paper, on which each subscriber shall put down the acres of land or the dollars in money he or she is willing to give, on condition that the whole assessed value of the territory shall be subscribed. When the subscription equals that value, then petition the Legislature to incorporate a board of curators of State parks, to manage this and all other State parks similarly constituted, under proper and specific regulations, and accountable to the State, but never to receive salaries or perquisites. If there should be any proprietors unwilling to sell for the assessed value, the State will exercise its right of eminent domain, and they will have their constitutional remedy in the courts.

The regulations of such a park that naturally suggest themselves are:—

1. That a large tract shall be kept as nearly as possible in a state of nature, and devoted to the studies of botany, ornithology, zoölogy, geology, and natural history in general, under the special care of distinguished naturalists, and not accessible to any without special permission.

2. That another large part should be open to the public as a park of recreation, in which individuals may establish such places of amusement and refreshment as the curators may approve, under the watch and care of a police whose indispensable qualification shall be politeness. And the curators shall exact such license fees for these places as shall defray the expenses of the police.

3. No tree shall ever be destroyed till it is dead or obstructs the growth of better trees.

4. The curators may let suitable sites to schools of horticulture, forestry and any special studies of natural history on such terms as will serve to defray the expense of desirable improvements in the park.

5. As it will be necessary to have many new names to distinguish particular localities in so extensive a park, I would, with the utmost deference, suggest that the hill on which we stand should be called Mount Andrew, and the whole territory Mount Andrew Park, in honor of one of the best-beloved Governors of Massachusetts; and the beautiful sheet of water on the left, Lake Winthrop, in honor of its discoverer. For the rest, as there are about as many hills in this 4,000 acres as there will be subscribers to the purchase, I propose that the largest subscription should give the right to the first choice of a hill, to which the subscriber may attach a name which shall be recognized on all future maps of the park;

and the next largest subscription shall entitle to the next choice, and so on.

As in the multitude of counsellors there is more safety than there can be in any individual, further suggestions on my part are needless. I will only say that if such an association is formed for this great purpose they may put me down for at least sixty-five acres, if they choose to include so much of my territory in the park.

The second plan is that proposed by Wilson Flagg. It takes the form of a joint stock company, and its separate provisions are as follows:—

1. The proprietors of the Middlesex Fells agree to form themselves into a joint stock company. For this end the whole region shall be appraised, each part according to its taxable valuation, or to a valuation by officers to whom the work may be delegated.

2. Every person who, according to this valuation, owns one thousand dollars in the land shall be entitled to one share in the joint stock, and to additional shares by the same rule.

3. If there be fractions over the value of shares to which any proprietor is entitled, the value of these fractions shall be credited to the owners, and the amount paid to them out of the fund that may be collected by the future sale of shares.

4. Persons who do not own property in the Fells may purchase shares, and the sums paid for them shall be funded, and out of this fund those proprietors shall be paid who wish to sell their property without joining the company.

5. It must be understood that any original proprietor who places his property into the common stock does not relinquish it, except that when he sells it he must sell only to the company, but may sell his shares to any person.

6. If any person who owns a little farm or homestead is willing to place his property in the common stock, but still wishes to occupy, he shall not be disturbed, nor shall he pay rent, until he shall receive the full value of his estate in money.

7. The intention is that no poor man shall suffer any damage or inconvenience by joining the company. After this he will be exempted from taxation, and may continue to occupy his house and farm as before, with certain restrictions in regard to cutting wood.

The act of incorporation may be as follows: —

1. This company shall be called the Middlesex Fells Institute.

2. The object of the company is to preserve a certain wild region situated chiefly in Stoneham and Medford, and called the Middlesex Fells, in its primitive condition for all time.

3. Also to secure the grounds from devastation, and to keep them as an asylum for our birds and other harmless animals, and a conservatory for all our indigenous plants.

4. The place shall also be a living museum of natural history and a practical school for the study of nature.

5. As the object of the company is educational and one of public benefaction, all that part of the region which is devoted to these purposes shall be exempt from taxation.

6. The officers of the company shall be a president, a vice-president, a secretary and treasurer and directors, to be chosen by the stockholders; also a superintendent and other officers, who shall be appointed by the president and directors.

7. No stockholder shall be assessed or taxed in any form for the benefit of the institution. All money paid by the stockholders shall be voluntary contributions.

"MIDDLESEX FELLS."

[*Massachusetts Ploughman*, Nov. 6, 1880.]

The Middlesex Fells Association propose to buy for a public domain a tract of about six square miles, or nearly four thousand acres, to be devoted to forest culture and preservation, science, education and rational recreation. Thirteen hundred and forty-four acres, or a little over two square miles, is in the northern part of Medford, and with the buildings on it is assessed on the tax list of the town at $90,603. Nearly four square miles are in the town of Stoneham, including Spot and Doleful Ponds, which occupy three or four hundred acres, the taxable value of which is yet to be ascertained. The eastern and western boundaries are rocky and precipitous hills, almost continuous, the eastern being in the towns of Malden and Melrose, and the western in Winchester. The latter town has a beautiful artificial lake as a reservoir for its water supply, which is included in the proposed forest park. The great advantage of this enterprise is that it will enrich the future without imposing any debt upon it.

THE GROWTH OF TREES.

[*Massachusetts Ploughman*, Dec. 9, 1880.]

Trees record their own history. The stump not only tells the age, but in what years the departed grew vigorously and in what it did little more than hold its own. I not long ago, in Ohio, measured the stump of a sugar maple, recently cut, and found it 30 inches in diameter. The tree had lived 125 years. In the first 63 years, while it stood in the dense forest, it had acquired but 9 inches in diameter. After the forest was cut away and it was left with only a few scattering companions, it soon assumed a superior rate of growth which it maintained till nearly the last, so as to add 21 inches of diameter in 62 years. The rings averaged about 17 hundredths of an inch in thickness, whereas in the first 63 years they had averaged but 7 hundredths.

In Sweden it is ascertained that a forest of mixed wood on medium soil grows about a cord of wood a year on an acre of land. If much more than a cord is removed from an acre in a year, the production is reduced. But to keep the production from diminishing it makes all the difference in the world what trees you take away, whether you take those which are beginning to decay, or those which are in the rapidest stage of growth. It is only by the best judgment in thinning out, that the capital of growth can be kept whole, after a forest has become well established.

If we take two trees of the same species, say an oak sapling, that is 4 inches in diameter, and 16 years old, and 20 feet high, and a tree that is 24 inches in diameter, 96 years old and 60 feet high, a little calculation will show us, supposing the thickness of the rings now equal, that the sapling is making 2.18 of a cubic foot of wood in a year, while the tree is making 3.924 cubic feet in a year. It will take between 32 and 33 such large trees on an acre to make a cord of wood in a year. And it will take about 590 of the saplings, or nearly four to the square rod. And it would take more than 70 to be cut to make a cord, so that in so young a forest a cord a year can not be taken away without trenching on the capital. It is not in fact till a forest is made, 100 years old, that it can yield so much as a cord an acre, without trenching on the capital of growth. But when it gets of that age, if the right care is taken, the average cord it yields is much more valuable than mere fire wood. The larger and more perfect the sound tree, the more valuable per cubic foot.

The forest I have supposed, consisting of 32 two foot trees to the acre, would make only between 40 and 50 cords of wood to the acre, if all cut at once. But that would be a destruction of capital which it would take nearly 100 years to restore, a capital which if kept up by replacing every tree cut, will continue forever to yield a net profit of at least ten dollars per acre yearly.

A forest, not to be ruined, must be managed very much as death manages the human race. Trees must not be taken out faster than they spring up, nor all of one age or sex, only those that are ripe, sickly and in the way. By adopting the species to the soil, even the poorest soils will yield immense returns. The rocky hills of Massachusetts which will not grow very large oaks or walnuts, will cover themselves with enormous pines and hemlocks, if they have an opportunity. As evergreens do not, like other trees, perpetuate themselves by sprouts from stumps, when a forest of them is slaughtered by the axe, their tender seedlings are prevented from replacing them by the sun, frost and cattle, while the hardier seedlings of the deciduous woods, such as birch, maple and ash, and the sprouts of such oaks and hickories as may have been mixed with the evergreens, have a better chance, and thus take the place of the resinous woods on a soil not so well adapted to them. With a little judicious care and forethought a wood of scrubby oak or hoop pole hickory may be converted into a glorious pinery, yielding masts for navies. But as the individual man has, on the average, a life shorter than that of a tree, it requires the State, which does not die, to do this.

The Middlesex Fells, so called, is a tract of nearly 4,000 acres within six or seven miles of Boston, of which more than 3,000 consist of rocky and blue gravel hills, once covered with lofty pines and hemlocks, nearly all of which have given place to oaks and hickories living lives of semi-starvation, and devastated by frequent forest fires.

There are about 140 proprietors, assessed, at an aggregate sum, between $200,000 and $300,000, and deriving an income from the fuel of a good deal less than one per cent. over the taxes. And this is taking annually more than is replaced, so that the tract, in spite of its woody green foliage in summer, and rainbow tints in autumn, is growing every year more desolate. Its condition, considering its capabilities, is really a disgrace to Middlesex County, and Suffolk as well.

It has been proposed that the citizens of the towns within whose territory this mostly unoccupied tract lies, and others interested in forest culture, should purchase this tract and give it to the State for the purpose of inaugurating a scientific and common-sense system of care for the trees. Should this be done, plainly in a hundred years from now the State might be enjoying from this tract alone a revenue of $30,000 a year, while it would be a source of health and recreation quite beyond the power of money to measure.

THE MIDDLESEX FELLS.

[*Medford Mercury*, Feb. 4, 1881.]

People are beginning to inquire, "What is the meaning of "fells"? Webster says a fell is "a barren or stony hill." He also says a feller is "one who fells or knocks down." Isaiah, speaking of the king of Babylon, says: "The fir trees rejoice at thee, and the cedars of Lebanon, saying, Since thou art laid down, no feller has come up against us." The trouble with our "Middlesex Fells" has been too many fellers. These fells, like any other fells, and there are more than a million acres of them in Massachusetts, can yield nothing of any account but trees. Yes, if these fells, all over the state, were ironed out smooth, there would be nearly two millions of acres. They are parcelled out by title deeds among about 50,000 little kings of Babylon. What I mean is, that there are not probably more than fifty farmers in the state who really know how to get the greatest yield of timber and fuel from a wood lot, or are sufficiently above hand-to-mouth poverty to get it if they did know how. As a rule the fells are trampled over and browsed on by cattle, and cut off clean for fire-wood as soon as the trees are one-fourth grown. Individual life is too short for the average farmer to have the care of woodlands. Every individual in the state has really an interest in every tree. The state, which does not die, can manage the woodlands so as to get, in a hundred years, four times the annual income from them, while it will certainly make them four times as beautiful, and more effective in preventing the water we need to drink from running into the sea.

But how shall the state government be made to see this? I can see no better way than for the people who surround the Middlesex Fells, and know the nature and history of this woodland tract of about 4,000 acres, to put their shoulders to the wheel and give it to the state for an experiment.

Speaking of putting shoulders to the wheel reminds me that in this country when people want anything done they are apt to call lustily on the Herculean Legislature without putting their own shoulders to the wheel. The Latin poet, Rufus Festus Avienus, wrote an excellent fable on this subject, which has become very popular in France, and I will close by quoting an English version of the French paraphrase.

   A Phaeton who drove a load of hay
    Once found his cart bemired.
   Poor man! the spot was far away
    From human help — retired
   In some rude country p'ace;
   In Brittany, as near as I can trace,
    Near Quimper Corentin,—
   A town which poet never sang,—
Which Fate, they say, puts in the traveller's path,
When she would rouse the man to special wrath.
May heaven preserve us from that route!
But to our carter, hale and stout:—
   Fast stuck his cart; he swore his worst,
   And, filled with rage extreme,
   The mud-holes now he cursed,
    And now he cursed his team,
    And now his cart and load,
    Anon, the like upon himself bestowed.

  Upon the god he called at length,
  Most famous through the world for strength;
   O help me Hercules cried he;
    For if thy back of yore
    This burly planet bore,
   Thy arm can set me free.
This prayer gone up, from out a cloud there broke
A voice which thus in god-like accents spoke: —
   The suppliant must himself bestir,
   Ere Hercules will aid confer.
  Look wisely in the proper quarter,
   To see what hindrance can be found;
  Remove the execrable mud and mortar,
   Which axle-deep, besets thy wheels around.
   Thy sledge and crow-bar take,
   And pry me up that stone, or break;
   Now fill that rut upon the other side.
   Hast done it ? Yes, the man replied.
   Well, said the voice, I'll aid thee now,
   Take up thy whip. I have, but how?
    My cart glides on with ease!
    I thank thee Hercules.
  Thy team, rejoined the voice has light ado;
  So help thyself, and Heaven will help thee too.

MIDDLESEX FELLS APPROACHES.

NORTHERN SUBURBS WAKING UP TO HAVE BOULEVARDS ACROSS
MYSTIC VALLEY.

[*Boston Herald*, March 3, 1881.]

Perfect roads, whether for locomotives or horses, for palace cars or for phaetons, coaches, buggies, sleighs, sleds or carts, are the best investments any city can make. They give equal pleasure and profit to men and animals, rich and poor; to the tired citizen who wishes to let his wife and children breathe the fresh air of the distant hills, and to the thrifty countryman who brings his load of fresh vegetables before sunrise to feed the city. The builders of the old milldam between Boston and the Brighton road "builded better than they knew," as any one who, at this day, takes his stand there on a pleasant afternoon, either in summer or winter, will plainly see. But the hitherto neglected Mystic valley can have for the making grander boulevards than can now be had at any price on the more populous side of our great city. The enterprising city of Somerville, I am happy to say, is beginning to open its eyes to this fact. The old historic town of Medford, famous for the ships it has built and for the "Cradock Mansion," built of English bricks, has already built a bridge of solid porphyry (named after that non-resident Governor), which will take a passenger across the Mystic, perhaps, without his knowing that he is on a bridge at all. It is now very nearly sure that, between the city of Somerville and the town of Medford, there will soon be the finest and most perfect roadway to be found in America. My reasons for this opinion are as follows:

1. That it will lead to one of the largest and most delightful parks in America. This park is not to be made, it already exists. It requires no art to beautify it. It only requires that science shall prevent art from spoiling it, and give nature an opportunity to restore some of the grand features which have been marred by thoughtlessness. It needs

to and must inevitably become a public domain, and, in fact, a Massachusetts park. Whether this takes place soon or late, there it is. As Daniel Webster said of Massachusetts, " Look at her."

2. That very road (I speak of the old Medford turnpike) has been, perhaps, the very worst to be found so near a great city in America. I am not alone in that opinion, as will appear from the following words, quoted from the 17th report of the state board of agriculture (p. 257):

" Probably the heaviest tax paid by the people of Massachusetts is that which they pay, in one form or another, for the privilege of maintaining some of the worst roads in existence.

" At this season, one may see anywhere in the country the proofs of paying this tax.

" Indeed, within 10 miles of this city (Boston), where we are in the habit of thinking that the arts of civilization are tolerably well understood, the traveller will find great county roads, like that leading through Somerville to Medford for example, over which there is constant and important transportation, which are in such disgraceful condition that they might reasonably be the subject of indictment."

Now, when, within five miles of a great city, two miles of a road, capable of being made, at a minimum of cost, not only the most useful but the most beautiful outlet into the country, has proved itself both a bottomless, perennial tax, and a nuisance worthy of indictment, to suppose that the cities and towns concerned in it will not wake up to make it what it might be, and ought to be, is to suppose that they are inhabited mostly by paupers or people who are not wise. This supposition is untenable. The cheapest thing to do will at last be done, and that is to make a road too solid to be worn out with any loads, or to be converted into mire by any weather, and beautiful enough to attract all sorts of travel. Such a road, being in such a place, whatever it costs, will pay, because it will raise the value of property at both ends, and be exempt from the unlimited tax, to which the author of the paper just quoted from in the agricultural report refers.

The old Medford turnpike, called of late Mystic avenue, was, if I am not mistaken, laid out in 1866 by the county commissioners to be a public road 66 feet wide. It has now been built more than half that, and so unscientifically as to have become the costly nuisance above described. The line for two miles is a dead level. The land on either side, if not freely given, can be bought very cheap, to improve it to any desirable width, by planting trees, and making it as attractive for pleasure travel as it will be useful for transportation.

The same improvements are applicable, and, doubtless, before long will be applied to Middlesex avenue, which branches off from Mystic avenue a little east of the new Somerville park, a plan very creditable to the enterprise of that young city. This new Middlesex avenue crosses the Mystic river on a trestle bridge just west of the Boston & Maine Railroad, passes through the sparse but neat village of Wellington, touches a corner of Everett and becomes Highland or Spot Pond avenue when it crosses the Malden line. This avenue is not a hard road to travel even now, and is finished into the Fells as far as Elm street. If continued straight across that street, it would strike Spot Pond at its southern extremity, then meeting Forest street, the old Andover turnpike, long since a free road, at nearly the exact centre of the proposed Forest Park. If continued a quarter of a mile beyond Forest street, it would reach the top of a truncated cone, or elliptical table land, where, without alighting from the carriage, one can overlook nearly the whole of the Fells, with its three beautiful sheets of water, and the spot where another is destined soon to be.

I am happy to say that some 70 of the prominent taxpayers of Somerville have petitioned its city government to complete at once its share of Mystic avenue to the width of 66 feet, and I have no doubt that the taxpayers of Medford, aroused by this example and having even a still deeper interest in the improvement, will follow suit.

THE PROPOSED SUBURBAN PARK BETWEEN MEDFORD AND STONEHAM.

[*Boston Daily Advertiser*, March 15, 1881.]

The desirability of reproducing the forest on the rocky hills between Medford and Stoneham has been generally recognized. It has been re-echoed from the western prairies. Boston's opportunity is the envy of a hundred cities. Every city may have a park, or a Shaw's garden (like St. Louis), but only Boston can have within five miles a forest of 4,000 acres, on the site of an ancient Laurentian volcano, whose centre is occupied by a crystal fountain of 400 acres.

Agriculture attacked that spot more than a hundred years ago, with its hatchets, hoes, and cobble-stone walls, and had to give it up. The woods grew again, but the axe has always been making ruthless havoc. Trees being the only living objects that can guarantee pure air and pure water for the benefit of mankind, and being good for the eyes and to make men wise, every individual of our teeming population has an interest in having the Middlesex Fells made sacred for the benefit of all.

How can it be done? This is a free country. We have no William the Conqueror to make a royal forest, which a cat may look at as well as a king. We have no czar, and we are glad of it. Any one of some 200 proprietors in the Fells may cut every tree and shrub within his lines when he pleases. If any individual or company should undertake to buy out all these proprietors, their prices for lots, hardly worth the taxes, would rise to the most ridiculous altitude. The State only, in general court assembled, has the right of eminent domain. But the State cannot be expected to act in the direction of making this a public forest, secured to all the well-behaved, unless the surrounding property, which will be more than doubled in value by the act, will indemnify the dispossessed proprietors, at least to the assessed value of what they relinquish. The assessed value of all that should be included in the domain does not exceed $300,000, while the real estate of the abutting towns is assessed at over $25,000,000. And the cities that will enjoy that forest, in every cell of their expanding lungs,— they and their multiplying posterity,— make the expense less than the dust of the balance.

What the Fells can be made, or rather what they will make of themselves with only letting alone, can be seen in two or three spots, and particularly on the Ravine Road, leading from Wyoming station, on the Boston & Maine Railroad, to Mr. John Botume's on Spot Pond.

This road passes through a lot of a little over thirty acres, covered with a noble growth of white pine, with scattered hemlocks. Any doctor who ever healed so many lungs should be proud. Doré would be delighted to see it.

The Middlesex Fells Association would be glad to enlarge its membership and its means of calling attention to this important movement. It has already started a conditional subscription of land within the Fells and money to indemnify for what land is not subscribed. It is not proposed to canvass for subscribers, but every member of the following committee will receive subscriptions on the condition that neither land shall be conveyed nor money paid till the legislature has passed an act taking possession of the entire tract under proper regulations for a forest park.

Committee — John Owen, Wilson Flagg, Cambridge; Lyman Dike, J. W. McDonald, Stoneham; Edwin A. Eaton, Elizur Wright, Boston; Jacob W. Manning, Reading; S. W. Twombly, Winchester; Lorin L. Dame, Medford; Mrs. P. D. Richards, West Medford; S. Baxter, R. Frohock, Malden; Miss H. Lynde, G. W. Reynolds, Melrose.

The success of this enterprise is of course more important to some of us than to others. But none of us who call Boston and its vicinity our home can afford to have it fail, and the aim of this little association is to enlist all the wisdom, wealth and energy necessary to make it a success in the shortest possible time.

A PAGE NOT POETRY.

Copied from the Massachusetts *Ploughman* and given here as representing statistical testimony at the time of these Appeals. 1980 can only have a better showing through the political wisdom, practical generosity and patriotism of to-day.

"The census report for 1880, which is the tenth in our history, shows that we have 25,708 establishments for converting the trees of our forests into lumber; that the sum of $14,181,122 is employed as the needful capital for carrying on this work, and that the value of the lumber produced is $233,367,729. From the twenty-third Forestry Bulletin, issued from the census office, we learn that the consumption of wood for fuel in the United States during the year of the census — 1880 — is estimated at 145,778,137 cords, of the value of $321,962,373. Of this quantity 140,537,490 cords were used for domestic purposes; 1,971,813 cords by the railroad; 787,862 cords by the steamboats; 358,074 cords in mining and amalgamating the precious metals; 266,771 cords in other mining operations; 1,157,522 cords in the manufacture of brick and tile; 540,448 cords in the manufacture of salt; and 158,208 cords in the manufacture of wool. During the same year, 74,008,972 bushels of charcoal were burned the value of which was $5,276,736.

These statistics are sufficient to show with what a wasteful celerity the destruction of our forests is proceeding, and that it must be stopped as far as possible, and repaired to the utmost, or we shall shortly become a treeless country, and therefore unproductive in any ratio with our present hopes and calculations. The *Northwestern Lumberman* of Chicago, reviewing the lumber production for the present year, says that 'to own a saw mill to-day, with ten years supply of standing timber, is to have that which is far better and safer than a gold mine in the Occident.' It also makes the statement that, the amount of timber cut from the forests of the northwest — Michigan, Wisconsin and Minnesota — in the year 1881, counting with the lumber, what was made into shingles was more than 7,000,000,000 feet; and adds that it takes some little grasp of the subject to comprehend so enormous a sum. If loaded on cars green, it would make a train nearly seven thousand miles in length; and the amount of money required to purchase it from first hands would be not far from $125,000,000. All this shows not only the necessity of tree-planting, but the pecuniary profit of it,— matters which must excite more attention every year."

OUR WATER SUPPLY.

ADDRESS DELIVERED IN THE TOWN HALL, MALDEN, ON THURSDAY EVENING, MARCH 31, 1881.

This terraqueous globe may be looked upon as a great water distillery, in which all land animals are deeply interested. The results are very differently distributed; the warmer climates, which most need water, being generally the best watered. But rain falls almost everywhere, more or less; even on the ocean, where it would seem to be needless for that great fish-bath would be kept equally fresh if all the rain fell on the land. On the land there are spots where rain seems never to fall, or to be evaporated as fast as it falls. Actual and careful observations show spots where the average annual rain-fall is only ten or twelve inches, and others, among tropical mountains, where it is ten or twenty times as much. Here it is about thirty-eight inches, but varying considerably in different years. Taking thirty-eight inches a year as what the grand celestial distillery allows to the people of Massachusetts, 857,655 imperial gallons of pure water in the course of a year fall on every acre. This is 2,355 gallons for every day. Hence, if we could somehow imprison this water on a space, say of 2,000 acres, so as to make it safe from those two grand marauders, gravity and evaporation, we should have a supply of 4,710,000 imperial gallons of water for every day in the year. This would supply drinking water for more than four millions of people, if they were not intemperate in that beverage, or it would supply more than forty thousand people with enough also to bathe themselves and their flowers and shrubbery.

There are, in the Middlesex Fells, full 2,000 acres, the rain-fall on which may easily be imprisoned against gravity and the omnivorous ocean. How far it can be imprisoned against evaporation depends a good deal on the reproduction of the forests that surround the natural and artificial reservoirs. Whatever the inroads of evaporation may be, and possibly they are quite capable, at their worst, of carrying off half the water that falls, they may be largely diminished by increasing the forests, for two reasons. First, forests shelter the surface from the sun, which is the great promoter of evaporation, and the more the denser they become. Second, they arrest the winds, which are also effective agents of evaporation. Dwarf or cut away the forests surrounding the reservoirs and the winds, having double or treble agitative force, fly away with two or three times as much water as they otherwise would.

When 250 years ago Gov. John Winthrop discovered this remarkable tract there were, doubtless, some rocks visible, for he named one "Cheese Rock." But most of them were hidden by dense and lofty forests of pine — the very best trees for the preservation of water. The trees stood on all the rocks except the scarps and huge boulders. Injudicious attempts at cultivation and short-sighted greed for fuel, in 250 years, have made most of the multitudinous hill-tops as bald as the skulls of a convention of boss politicians, or even of the present speaker. The ice-rivers of the last glacial period sweeping over these craggy rocks, left them not only treeless, but rounded and polished on their tops, with nothing for trees to grow on but the debris in the gorges, and here and there in the crevices that seamed the rocks.

Beginning in the valleys it must have taken hundreds of centuries for the forests to creep up to the tops of the hills, but they did it at last, and finally so covered the bare granite scalps with the decayed foliage of centuries, that pine seedlings could vegetate and throw their roots to every point of the compass till they found deep crevices by which to hold on and defy the storm. Then came civilized humanity, and with thoughtlessness and want of foresight utterly unworthy of its history and its brains, in less than three centuries, undid this sublime victory of vegetable life!

The only comfort is, that it is quite possible for civilization, in another 250 years, so to assist nature that she shall more than replace herself in her former grandeur.

The means of doing it are too obvious to all gardeners and foresters to need more than hinting at. And this is a case where the useful and the sweet are, as usual, in perfect harmony. If we are to have the largest and best water supply, the reservoirs or the storage of the water must be cleared, as far as possible, of all the soil and muck between the high and low water levels; and these substances, if placed where they are needed, will give a chance for pine seedlings to establish themselves on all the hill tops. In making new reservoirs every atom of muck, soil, or mud, no matter how deep, should be excavated and utilized. All trees, it is to be remembered, derive the greater part of their pabulum — that of which the wood is composed — from the atmosphere. They feed chiefly on the gases that are noxious to animal life. About all they require of the earth is means of holding on while they pump moisture enough for their sap. Give them that, and they will clothe the rockiest mountains with green up to the snow line. Here utility and beauty are indispensable to each other.

To create a purely ornamental park, like the Central Park of New York, is a matter of vast expense, over and above the cost of the site, but the proposed Middlesex Fells Forest Preserve will cost really nothing beyond the appraised value of the land and buildings included in it — and perhaps not so much. The trees it already has will pay for their preservation and increase, and at the end of a quarter of a century will yield a net income. With a comparatively trifling outlay to perfect the means of traversing this vast natural park, both on foot, on horseback, and on wheels, it will yield more pleasure and instruction than it is possible for any merely artificial park to do. There are already reasonably good carriage roads traversing the territory from north to south on each side of Spot Pond. Middlesex or Spot Pond Avenue which leads directly from Somerville Park to the junction of Elm and Fulton sts., if prolonged to Forest st. and a little way beyond, will have easily reached a remarkable eminence nearly in the centre, commanding a view of every sheet of water which is now, or may be, contained in it — not less probably than five of the loveliest lakes — Boston's net work of cities, towers, islands and ocean. That hill presents at the top an elliptical conic section of about four acres. The avenue, as a driveway, will be carried around its circumference and return into itself, forming a *cul de sac* better worth driving into than any other in America. Of course the interior of the ellipse should be covered with the loftiest pines, from the centre of which should rise, fifty feet or more above their tops, a watch tower of permanent and beautiful construction, with a steam elevator for the accommodation of visitors, and to pump up sufficient water for the irrigation of that and other high places. It is quite possible, without making any eye-sores, to have such structures very useful to guard against the forest fires, as well as to give a cheap, safe, and innocent amusement to all who admire fine landscapes. If the necessary buildings and towers are clothed in verdure, as they easily may be, the harmony of forest scenery will not be disturbed, and the most perfect and desirable contrast between city and wilderness will be preserved.

THE FORESTS.

[*Boston Journal*, Nov. 2, 1881.]

Your correspondent S. has done well to draw public attention to the Middlesex Fells, and to show what an opening is there for a corporation to serve the public and at the same time make a paying investment. He is quite correct, and the only wonder is that what he suggests was not done years ago.

Perhaps the first example of it will be in the State of Virginia. About a month ago I met in Chicago Mr. Cleaveland, the landscape gardener, well known in this city, and the creator of the South Park in that. He had just returned from Virginia, whither he had been called for consultation by a corporation which has purchased 2,000 acres, including the celebrated Natural Bridge, with the design of making a pleasure resort for the world. Mr. Cleaveland thinks the Middlesex Fells quite as valuable for a similar purpose. But the five adjoining towns, with a population of about 35,000, and a real estate valuation of over $25,000,000, have their eyes now fixed upon the " Fells " for a still more vital purpose, to wit, their water supply, which demands the highest possible prosperity of the forest surrounding it. They have a joint committee which will meet next Monday evening at the Town Hall in Medford to consider and report to the several towns what action it is best for the next town meetings to take in the matter. That committee may report against any action by the towns, or that these towns shall manage the Fells entirely on their own account, or that they shall ask the Legislature for a general act in regard to forests, under which all similar tracts shall be cared for by the Commonwealth, and a race of practical foresters shall be created, who shall do for forests taken under State guardianship what the farmers do for the agricultural crops. If this committee should report against any action, then a corporation will be in order; for anything is better than the ruthless ravages of the woodchoppers or the mercenary schemes of real estate speculators, some of whom have already divided about 80 acres into small village lots, of which more than 70 are said to have been sold. Happily no buildings have yet been erected on them. If there should be, the drainage will be directly into the water supply.

MEN AND TREES.

It is scarcely more than a century since the much persecuted Rev. Dr. Joseph Priestley discovered the chemical constitution of our atmosphere. Before that, men did not know what they were breathing.

For ages on ages they did not know that the air had weight or what made water rise in a pump. Now, thanks to Priestley and others, we know that the diluted oxygen we take into our lungs every moment carries off carbon in the shape of carbonic acid gas, which is poison for men but food for trees. The trees greedily devour the carbon of this gas, and liberate the oxygen, thus making it fit to be breathed again.

Chemists well know that the vegetable world is the mother of the animal, and without the constant vigorous life of the mother the offspring could not exist. Death is the lot of all animals.

But crowded, ill-ventilated halls, and dense ill-drained cities greatly hasten it for the human population. Why? Mainly by obliging the lungs to breathe again the poison they have just discharged, or the gases that have been vomited from thousands of furnace throats. Those gases, forests, wherever they exist, are ready to convert into wood, and restore the atmosphere to its normal purity.

Cities solicitously provide the modern conveniences, but the ancient convenience of neighboring forests, from which the balmy zephyrs can flood their streets with pure air, is worth untold sums. Our good old drowsy Commonwealth is not insensible to the value of health. It does not like to see its beautiful young sons and daughters fade away with consumption, in the very bud. So it authorizes its towns to make boards of health, and makes one itself, and clothes them with powers quite equal to their knowledge. Shall it not look to its forests a little, and exercise its right of *eminent domain* in their favor, when they are thirsting to drink up the poisons which would hurry our youth and beauty to the graveyard? Trees have rights which men, if they value their own right to life, liberty and the pursuit of happiness, are bound to respect. The individual man may not be able to recognize his relation to the individual tree, but the Commonwealth must appreciate its relation to forests or suffer.

THE NEW FOREST LAW.

[*Boston Transcript*, June 10, 1882.]

The Middlesex Fells agitation has resulted in a very suggestive, if not important, piece of State legislation (see chapter 255 of the Acts of 1882 — the same as House Document 358), giving towns and cities the right to take land to be devoted to forestry, on the same terms as for roads or streets. The title to such lands is then to vest in the Commonwealth. They are to be under the care of the State Board of Agriculture as a board of forestry, who will appoint skilful, practical foresters, to be paid out of the produce, and all surplus is to go to the municipalities ceding the lands. In a State where at least one-fourth of the land is fit for pine forests, and really for nothing else, this is legislation in the right direction. Evergreen forests grow principally out of the air, and as they absorb noxious gases in winter as well as summer, they purify the air more effectively even than the deciduous trees.

The Legislature having done its duty, it is now for the people themselves to consider what is theirs — what they owe to their posterity, if not to themselves. The question arises in our populous State, How shall we provide for the two great necessities of life — pure water and pure air? Our spindles, looms and sewing machines bring us bread, but add nothing to the purity of our water or our air — rather the reverse. Any sort of water will extinguish fires. Common river water will do for bathing, washing and many other purposes. But for drinking and cooking the people should have the purest possible, such as falls from the sky and filters into reservoirs not subject to pollution. Forests, if they can be reproduced and preserved, will greatly assist in securing such reservoirs.

Take for example the Middlesex Fells region, of about 4,000 acres, including hardly 200 fit for agricultural purposes, but which was once covered by lofty pines and hemlocks, and may be again. The water falling on at least 3,000 acres of it may be held in clean reservoirs, not subject to any pollution. That at present retained in the natural reservoir of Spot Pond is well known to be of the purest, though by dredging the marshes connected with it its purity may be improved. The average annual rainfall in our climate is said to be about thirty-eight inches, a large part of which goes off by evaporation or sudden floods, where it is not protected by forests. But suppose only twenty-four inches can be retained for human use, that on 3,000 acres — and so much of the Middlesex Fells might be made available for the purpose — would give in a year 1,628,820,000 imperial gallons, or enough to supply a population of 2,231,300 with *two gallons a day* for drinking purposes — or more than a million, if half of it should be wasted in freighting it to their mouths. Seeing that the remotest part of the Middlesex Fells is but eight miles from our City Hall, and Boston begins to tire of drinking Sudbury River, this matter has some interest for its population. Perhaps by an extension of pipes, and having two distinct systems of supply all round instead of one, a good deal of Sudbury might be exchanged for a smaller quantity of Spot Pond, without damage to the population of either Middlesex or Suffolk.

A LECTURE

DELIVERED TO THE WOMAN'S CLUB OF EAST BOSTON.

I understand this to be a Woman's Club. This word *club* has two distinct meanings, as it comes from two distinct sources, having not the slightest relation to each other — not so much, even, as a policeman's club has to a broomstick.

There is another word *cleave*, which also has two meanings, because from two sources. One is, to *split apart* and the other is, to *stick together*. *Club* comes from *cleave*, in the former sense, because the expense of the common object is *split* or shared between the members. Plainly it should claim the right to the latter sense by its cohesiveness or *sticking together*.

Man has had clubs innumerable, from time immemorial, some for good but more for bad. Clubs of women, for great and good purposes, are a new feature of society, and full of hope for better times. They have for their objects, to promote education, to form good habits and reform the bad, to purify and beautify life. This is a vast work, but many hands make it light.

Our home at present is on the planet we call earth. We sometimes call it mother earth. And really she is the mother of all the living that we know of. She is beautiful, grand and sometimes terrible, beyond the power of words. Her oceans are full of life, from the enormous leviathan to the invisible mollusk,— beings resplendent in form and color, which no human eye has ever seen. From her briny and gelid deeps come up swimmers that bask in the sunshine of her beaches, survey the dun waves with their great round eyes, rejoice in the gambols of their young, and then plunge into their spacious home. Her vast continents, with mountains, hills, valleys, broad plains, all bathed in blue sky, and overhung here and there with gorgeous cloud curtains, carpeted with emerald lit up with rainbow hues, under the sublime sunlight, are full of infinitely various life. In air, earth, and water everything lives, breathes and sleeps. The whole earth is alive with motion of swift feet and swifter wings. The great mother herself is swifter than all, as she whirls in the celestial dance, joyful and tireless, around the great centre of light, heat and force.

Of all the children of earth, man as a mere animal, is the most pitifully unfit for the terrible struggle to exist. The lion, the bear, the wolf, the rattlesnake, the scorpion, and countless other races, are either stronger or better armed. But man has a relatively larger brain, and more power of thought. He invents tools. Other animals have sharper senses. The eagle sees further with the natural eye. But man has invented the artificial eye, which can peer a million times further than the eagle's towards the infinitely great and the infinitely little.

After thousands and thousands of years of observation, experiment and thought, in spite of the shortness of human life and the myriads of enemies and obstacles that surround it, the human mind has succeeded in wresting from the great enigmatic nature of things two or three very important and fruitful secrets. To one of them I will presently call your attention.

. . . .

In regard to all forests, beauty, health and profit all go together hand in hand. Every forest will richly repay for its care by its superfluous growth — thinning out and taking away only those trees which have ceased to grow and letting younger ones take their place. This is a science which the old world has learned and is ready to teach us.

There may be other reasons why men have decayed and nations faded away. But the destruction of the forests alone is sufficient to account for the present scarcity and poor quality of men where a high civilization once existed. By denuding the hills of their natural clothing you dry up the streams and spoil the climate. There is no such thing as waste land. Trees will grow on any land not fit for a garden, whether it be swamp or rock. A white pine only asks anchorage, and will thrive on a rock very nearly bare. But when the land is parcelled out among people, not one of whom lives a hundred years, and most die by the time they are fifty, a forest is regarded as nothing but a wood-lot, and is butchered off every twenty or thirty years. It is thus made a mere burnt offering to the demon of ignorance. Trees that would go down to posterity, as the glorious patriarchs of many generations, are thus slaughtered in their teens, and the parched land knows them no more forever.

The forests are of the air, and really belong to the whole people, to all who breathe, as the air does. Metes and bounds cannot confine the delicious odor of the pines and the hemlocks, nor the glorious autumnal colors of the maple and the birches. Surely at least some of the forests should be the common property of some power or authority that is likely to live as long as trees do and be made the most of, for the benefit of great cities and populous towns.

And this brings me to the *Middlesex Fells*, and what can be done there to restore the pines, hemlocks, maples, beeches, oaks, ash and walnuts to their primeval glory, when they hid all the jagged rocks under their immense clouds of deep green foliage. That tract of nearly 4,000 acres, including 400 of water, has about 130 proprietors owning from 150 acres to half an acre. Lots of it have been sold, over and over, for taxes. Because the roads are so difficult many of the proprietors neglect to thin out their wood and leave it a prey to fire. Others sell it to the wood-chopper, who takes all he can and leaves the brush to burn up the young pines. As a forest it is in a most absurd and disgraceful condition, even a great deal worse than it looks. For even a scrub-oak hill always succeeds in looking pretty well at a distance. Nature only takes a year or two to cover decently the haggard nakedness which a ruthless Yankee wood-chopper leaves behind him. The General Court last winter, after a most thorough discussion of the matter, proposed an Act, by which the towns and cities may devote such part of their territory as they please to the reproduction and preservation of forests, compensating the proprietors in the same way as if the land were taken for roads or streets. Such land is to become a public domain, under regulations fixed by the Statute, the title to vest in the State, and the care of it to be taken by the State Board of Agriculture, as a Board of Forestry — which Board, of course will appoint suitable men to carry out the object of the law. The trees should have fit guardians, with knowledge in their heads and a proper worship of the beautiful in their hearts.

So it is reduced to a question of mere dollars and cents — and not more than *one-third of a million of dollars*, at that, whether Boston and its environs, embracing a population of half a million, including perhaps a score of millionaires, and all pretty well off, shall have almost within its very bosom the grandest lake-dotted forest belonging to any city in the world. The aggregate wealth of all the people directly interested, cannot be less than a thousand millions of dollars. They think nothing of making public improvements, under ground and above ground, which cost several millions. They are bound to have pure air as well as pure water, cost what it may. It is not the *cost* of making the Middlesex Fells a public domain, and a great people's forest, which stands in the way, it is only the *thought*, that is waiting to be waked up. It is an object, when once really looked at, to wake up the enthusiasm of the merest groundling.

Now if this woman's club takes any interest in the questions of how to get the purest water and the purest air; if it has, as it surely must have, a tender regard for the rosy little cherubs that are yet to be born by millions within this circle of twenty miles diameter, in the coming ages, here is some work for it. It is in the power of a club like this — I see it in their eyes — to set the whole city and surrounding country in a blaze — to convince everybody that what ought to be, must be and will be.

Why has this tract, fitted by nature to be a wonder of beauty — endlessly varied beauty — been left a waste for two hundred and fifty years, with hardly a dozen comfortable homes in it, and not more than two decent farms? Plainly to give the young people of this cultured and scientific age, an opportunity to do a nice thing, a glorious thing in the sight of coming centuries. Architects have done great things. Some of their buildings fill the mind with awe, or inspire it with a sense of power. But what are palaces, and domes to a forest with its living arches, telling of men who planted it hundreds of years ago? Doré can paint a forest that almost makes one feel cool in the dog days. But a real forest, intertwining its boughs in the sky, and absorbing the heat of the sun, makes a coolness which is far more refreshing and more fragrant. In such places is where genius is born, if anywhere. Art will then go to school to Nature herself. . . .

Possibly it may be true, as some have contended, and some disputed, that plants give out some carbonic acid in the night. But what of carbon they lose in the night compared with what they gain in the daytime, must be less than what a healthy infant loses of milk when that is furnished abundantly compared with what it absorbs and assimilates. As a dominant and demonstrated fact, trees do nothing to the air, to speak of, but to purify it for the use of animals, and most of all for the use of men, women and children, who are the animals that have most need of pure air.

Every animal that breathes — and the more so the higher its temperature — has a circulating fluid which by a pumping engine called the heart is constantly driven through a set of branching pipes to every part of the body, carrying with it the nutriment prepared by the laboratory of the stomach which is necessary to the growth of every part, or its repair, — for the action, whether of body or mind, is constantly putting every part out of repair. Repair always implies waste. This waste consists of various materials, and physiology shows various means by which they are got rid of, the correct action of all of which are essential to breathe; but I need speak of only one of these waste materials, which appears to be simple carbon, in an inconceivably minute state of division — that wonderful element which sometimes sparkles as a diamond and oftener looks blacker than night while ready to turn night into day by its combustion. There is another set of tubes — waste pipes, called veins which lead from every part of the body through that double action pump the heart to the lungs, and we account for the darker color of the blood in these waste pipes, than that of the other set of ducts called arteries, by their absorbing waste carbon. This one fact of the darker color of venous blood would not prove the presence of carbon. But when some of it is put in a bottle containing pure oxygen and shaken, it instantly turns as red as arterial blood, and the air in the bottle which was before pure oxygen, is now partly carbonic acid gas. So when air is inhaled into the lungs, without a particle of carbonic acid in it, but only oxygen diluted with nitrogen, a good deal of carbonic acid comes out with the next outward breath, or exhalation, and it is known that the blood which comes out of the lungs into the heart, is lighter and brighter colored than that which was pumped by the heart into the lungs. But here comes an apparent difficulty. The venous blood pumped so forcibly into the lungs cannot possibly mix with the air inhaled into them — and be shaken up with it — unless the party is bleeding at the lungs. But we get over this difficulty by a little observation and thought. All animal and vegetable tissues or membranes, like the artificial tissues of our looms, are pervious strainers to what is fine enough to go through. The multitudinous air cells of the lungs among which the venous blood is pumped by the heart with some force, have probably no pores or interstices in their walls which can ever be discovered by any microscope, yet there must be such as will let the atoms of carbon through, without letting through the corpuscles of the blood, and especially when oxygen is inside to welcome the carbon atoms into chemical union. The passage and intermixture of fluids and gases of different densities is known to take place through even dead membranes, and the now well-known terms *endosmosis* and *exosmosis* are used to describe the facts. The life principle, power or force is constantly working in this way both in animals and vegetables, men and trees, and they die the moment it ceases so to work.

At any rate, whether we can explain the fact or not, it certainly is the fact, that all animal life is constantly producing and throwing into the atmosphere carbonic acid gas, which it cannot breathe with impunity either pure or mixed in any considerable proportion with common air. Were it not for vegetable life, which absorbs this carbonic acid gas, appropriates its carbon and renders back to the air its oxygen, animal life would hardly be possible. And geologists tell us that vegetable life, to a vast amount, actually preceded all but the lowest forms of animal life. It was the process by which the carbonic acid gas which must at first have formed a large part of the atmosphere was condensed into the coal beds, and thus the world was prepared for the habitation of beings who could learn how to burn coal and raise steam. And now the more they burn coal, the more they need trees to absorb the carbonic acid gas which results from combustion as well as breathing.

Search beneath the crust of this planet has discovered on all its continents and large islands large deposits of coal — by no means, however, unlimited. The manufacturing arts are using it up at such a rate that in a few centuries it must be exhausted. Nothing but the growth of forests can insure us against exactly such a state of the atmosphere as must have existed before vegetation had purified it by depositing the coal beds — a condition fatal to the human race, or any race of animals perhaps except the cold-blooded. Hence the welfare of mankind is bound up in the prosperity of the forests. Of course we may expect forests to grow naturally very much in proportion to the pabulum of carbonic acid thrown into the air, but still human wisdom and foresight may be and ought to be an important factor in making that growth sufficient and seasonable. The salvation from the forests will be too late for the men who are first suffocated.

It would require volumes to set forth all the hygienic

virtues of forests. History shows how nations have suffered for sweeping them away. But for the hills and mountains that scorn the plough, the industry of man would perhaps before this have made the whole earth a desert and relegated all life to the ocean. Trees, silent and self-adjusting as they are, are the best friends of man, and forests alone can save great cities.

I have dwelt thus prolixly, and I fear tediously, on the physically hygienic influence of forests because it is a vital and all-important fact, and will become more and more so as population increases and modern civilization progresses. The destruction of the forests is the terrible lee shore of our civilization — the rocks ahead.

I will advert now to the hardly distinguishable head, the æsthetic or moral influence of forests. Whatever attracts the sense of beauty, order, harmony, variety in the mind not only elevates and ennobles the moral character, but contributes to the physical health. A grand forest, multitudinous trees, all towering aloft in glorious rivalry to greet and share the sunlight — no quarrelling, no cheating, no meanness — sheltering the poor animals from biting cold as well as blistering heat — there you have the nurse — the *alma mater* — of human genius. Through eye, ear and every subtler sense, the very milk of the soul is poured into every possible poet. Must not men and women first feel before they can express feeling? There are a thousand who can feel poetry, where there is one that can express it in words, or on canvas. But the grand thing is to feel it and live it. A primeval forest of three or four thousand acres accessible to every man, woman and child, will poetize a great city. Try it and see. Such a forest with a variety of trees and shrubs is a vegetable democracy. It typifies a state of human society, possible, but never yet attained by the human race, wherein without domineering or supplanting dwell harmoniously people of all sorts of talents each in the sphere best suited to them. Every tree minds its own business, gets its own living by its own force of character, and only occupies space according to the multitude of leaves with which it blesses the eyes and the lungs of all that breathe.

Forests not only purify the air, but they have a most important and practical relation to the purity and preservation of fresh water. Fresh and pure water is scarcely less necessary to the chemical laboratory of the stomach, than pure air to the lungs. Civilization, culminating in vast, crowded cities, is at its wits' end to supply this necessity. It builds great aqueducts above or underground, to convey distant rivers and distribute the water to every dwelling. And, after all, perhaps the water is only diluted sewage. Rivers naturally carry all sorts of filth to the sea, making provision there for the fertility of continents that may emerge a million of years hence. To have water fit for drinking and culinary purposes, we must resort to springs, whose water has been filtered through the earth, or to cisterns catching pure water from the sky. Family cisterns are insufficient, if not impracticable, in a crowded city shrouded in smoke and redolent of all sorts of gases. But a city with a million of people, which has an elevated water-shed of 4,000 acres, outside of its dust and smoke, may have a cistern which will supply every mouth with all the pure water it needs to swallow, provided trees instead of men occupy the whole surface of the water-shed except the reservoirs. A forest uses a little water itself, but it prevents the evaporation and waste of vastly more than it consumes. Only consider, that in our climate about 38 inches of water fall in a year, on the average. This makes the average rainfall on 4,000 acres, about 3,438,600,000 imperial gallons in a year. Allowing one-half for absorption by the trees, evaporation and waste, there would remain $4\frac{7}{1000}$ imperial gallons per day for a million of mouths. With total abstinence from all other liquids would not this be enough? If not, let us have other forest water-sheds. Massachusetts has hills enough, if they were only clothed with pines, to save any possible population of her valleys from the necessity of imbibing sewage in any state of dilution.

It is needless to say that the human being is the crowning glory of the animal world. If not conscious of it, we are all educated to that faith. It is equally needless to say that there is before the human race vast room for greater elevation both physical and intellectual, individually and collectively. So in the vegetable world there is room for improvement — there is vast variety of character there — some plants are eminently friendly to us, while others, like some of the animals, are hostile or deadly. All the friendly look to us for protection and improvement. Their welfare is linked with ours. We need to study the vegetable world, including the mineral on which it lives, for our own sakes as well as its. For example, there is a single plant which has established the most intimate relations with civilized as well as savage man, which presents a field for the most profound study. It presents a great practical problem, of wide moral and financial bearings, hardly second in importance to any now before the civilized world. And what is probably true of it is, that every individual will have to decide it for himself. I do not say herself, for the female sex, seems pretty generally to have decided, or solved the problem for itself already. Poets, philosophers and statesmen, of the male sex, seem still in doubt. Charles Lamb, though he denounced the plant as "filth of mouth and fog of mind" still sang its praise in bewitching verse. Can there be a stronger argument for the study of botany, based as it is on mineralogy, chemistry and geology, and connected with zoölogy, and particularly with the natural history of insects and birds? And what can possibly be a better school apparatus for such studies than a "public domain" of 4,000 acres, within a half hour's ride of the city, with a varied forest, growing on one of the oldest and wildest volcanic upheavals on this part of the continent?

"MIDDLESEX FELLS."

[*Massachusetts Ploughman*, June 10, 1882.]

On the 17th of June there is to be a meeting, at "Cheese Rock," in the "Middlesex Fells," of the Fells Association and the Essex and Middlesex Institutes; and everybody else who feels an interest in their common purpose, which is the preservation of our forests, is invited to be present. More than usual enthusiasm may be looked for in the meeting, seeing that the new Forest Law has been promulgated as an act of the Legislature. It has been truly observed that the Legislature has done its duty in relation to the forests of the State, and it is now the part of the people to do theirs. The new Forest Law may with perfect truth be said to be the result of the agitation that was begun by the Middlesex Fells Association. It is esteemed as important a piece of legislation as has been performed in many years. We of this generation cannot reasonably expect to see and enjoy the full fruits of it, but they will begin to fairly outline the noble prospect of the future to us before all of us go hence and leave a grateful posterity to enjoy what we have considerately done. Massachusetts has set a worthy example in the step she has just taken, which can scarcely fail to be followed by the other States.

The new law gives to towns and cities authority to take all lands which they may deem proper to devote to forestry, the lands to be paid for to their owners on the same terms as lands taken for streets and roads now are. After they have been taken for this purpose, the titles to them rest absolutely in the State, and are to come under the care of the State Board of Agriculture, which is to constitute a Board of Forestry, and by which skilful, expert, and practical foresters are to be appointed, to be paid from the natural products of the forests themselves. If there is any surplus, as there certainly will be a steadily increasing one, it is to go to the treasury of the towns and cities thus ceding the lands to the

State. It is fairly estimated that fully one-fourth of all the land in the State is adapted only to pine forests. This fact is enough to impress on all minds the importance of the law just enacted. The growth of evergreen forests may be regarded as peculiarly fit for this climate, flourishing, as they do, equally in the winter and the summer. In a country thus clad the climate is notably a healthy one, the air being in process of constant purification. Evergreen forests protect the deciduous trees, and both combine to furnish needed shelter to the crops of the field and the garden.

THE LEGEND OF "CHEESE ROCK,"

FOR THE FOREST FESTIVAL, JUNE 17, 1882.

In sixteen hundred thirty-one,—
    It was a winter day,—
When Winthrop, Nowell, Eliot,
    To northward strolled away.

The frozen Mistick flood they crossed,
    Ere Cradock's mansion stood;
O'er swamps and rocky hills they pressed,
    Through miles of lofty wood.

They crossed a lovely ice-bound lake,
    With islands here and there;
" SPOT POND " they called it, from the rocks
    That showed their noddles bare.

Then up northwestwardly they climbed
    A hill well crowned with trees,
And hungry there, as well might be,
    They dined on simple cheese.

For, why, the guv'nor's man in haste,
    And careless how they fed,
His basket loaded with the cheese,
    And quite forgot the bread.

This fact, so simple and so grand,
    To us they handed down;
" CHEESE ROCK " they named that lovely hill,
    Those men of high renown.

Some smaller men cut off the trees,
    And then they named it " Bare ";
And when the bushes wildly grew,
    They spelled it " B-e-a-r."

But Nature still asserts her rights
    Against all vulgar spells,

And cries aloud, " Restore the pines
To these my favorite Fells.

" Mount Winthrop you may call this spot,
If you'll preserve the trees
That canopied with winter's green
The guv'nor's lunch of cheese!"

THE MIDDLESEX FELLS.

[*Massachusetts Ploughman*, June 17, 1882.]

Since the passage of the Forest Law, [chapter 255 of the Acts of 1882] the destiny of the "Middlesex Fells," so called from the peculiar abruptness of the surface, has become a subject of great interest to the entire commonwealth. That region, of which Spot Pond is nearly the centre, is doubtless of volcanic formation, and a body of pure water now occupies the place where once the force of fire threw the surrounding rocks into fantastic shapes, which the succeeding ice floods did not entirely obliterate. The glacial drift arrested by the sharp volcanic prominences was too scanty for the sustenance of any forest trees except the hardy conifers which grow chiefly from the air. Accordingly our ancestors found these fells clothed chiefly with pines and hemlocks, which they attacked without mercy, and attempted to replace with apple trees. But after honey-combing three or four thousand acres with stone walls, and finding the stones still as plenty as ever, they retreated from the volcanic region pretty much, and left it to grow up to what is called "wood-lots." These are by no means profitable if the growth is left to chance and fire, and the crop of wood is treated like a crop of rye, and cut off smooth every twenty or thirty years.

Agriculture cannot be complete unless forests are included in its scope. Hence the present law has wisely made the State Board of Agriculture a Board of Forestry also; provided any of the municipalities of the commonwealth shall cede land to the same for the purpose of being used for the reproduction and perpetual preservation of forest growth.

More than any other crop, that of trees needs the application of the highest science and skill to bring it to perfection. And as the life-time of the most valuable trees is more than twice that of man, the care of our forests, in which all are interested, cannot safely be left to individual proprietors, but only to the State, which is least expected to die. European experience has proved that forests, to yield the greatest and best product of timber, should never be destroyed, but only be thinned, by removing super-abundant and inferior trees, and those that have come to full maturity — at the same time planting successors.

The tract called the Middlesex Fells has quite distinct natural boundaries, and the whole belongs to Stoneham, Medford, Winchester, Melrose and Malden; the shares, as to extent of surface being in the order of the municipalities above named. In regard to the preservation and purity of the water supply, it is quite essential that the *public domain* should include all that naturally does or by art can be made to drain into Spot Pond or the Winchester or other possible artificial reservoirs. All population that could injure the forests or defile the water should be excluded. Were the five municipalities above named one, there could be no doubt that this, under the present law, would be done. If the thinking and leading people who live within ten miles of the fells will spend the 17th of this month in looking over them, it will certainly be done, and they will make 1882 hardly less memorable than 1774.

The only practical question is, whether the five municipalities can agree to avail themselves of the power granted them by this Forest Act. But every city and town within ten miles, as well as the entire State, is interested, and if this great forest festival is attended as it ought to be, not one of the five proprietor towns but will see that it cannot afford to dissent from an agreement. In fact, the greater its territory in the fells the stronger its motive to assent, if it will only look a little ahead. As to the profit of territorial possession, it is a clear case of a part being greater than the whole — a thing not unusual in agriculture, as all successful agriculturists know. The five towns interested tax themselves on about $25,000,000 of real estate, of which the value of that in the fells cannot exceed $350,000, or one and four-tenths per cent. It is clear enough that under the forest law they can make themselves richer, and the forest will make itself the delight if not the salvation of Massachusetts.

It is well known how a little science and private enterprise have in fifty years reared some beautiful pine forests on the Cape and elsewhere. It remains to see what the State Board of Agriculture can do on the rocks of Middlesex Fells — if it has the opportunity.

ADDRESS

DELIVERED AT THE FOREST FESTIVAL JUNE 17, 1882.

[*Massachusetts Ploughman*, June 24, 1882.]

Back of all that has been said is the great law of Nature, well ascertained and even taught in some of our school books, that the animal life of this planet depends upon the vegetable — man's upon that of the tree. The human animal, of all the most, requires an atmosphere of pure oxygen diluted with nothing but nitrogen. Possibly before the first gigantic forest growths had absorbed the carbon out of the atmosphere, making the vast coal formations, the saurian monsters may have managed to breathe, but men could not, if they had then existed. Nor can they long continue to exist, if they burn up the coal at the rate of 280,000,000 tons a year and destroy the forests. At least one-fourth of its territory should be devoted to forests, and sacredly guarded from fire or no extensive nation can long continue to exist. Every living man, woman or child is a small furnace constantly pouring carbonic acid into the atmosphere; and what can be depended on to decompose that deadly poison but the vegetables that feed on carbon? Water may absorb a little of the gas, and make it harmless and even invigorating as a drink; but we die if we breathe much of it. With a bad atmosphere good ventilation is of little account. A city, steepled all over with tall chimneys, may send its carbonic acid from a thousand furnaces high into the air, but much of it will settle down and come back into the houses — sending the rich to the White Mountains or across the ocean; but what shall become of the toilers who cannot go? That ci'y must have two or three large pine forests, within a few minutes' ride, where the most useful part of its population may occasionally breathe freely, or it will suffocate. Boston had better wake up to consider this subject practically, or for conscience' sake burn some of its school-books. Ornamental parks are nice things, and perhaps worth millions. But they cannot do the work of forests. The Assyrian empire perished soon after the forests in the valley of the Euphrates did. Nebuchadnezzar's beautiful hanging gardens could not save it.

O for a worthy psalm
To the pine, oak and palm!
To the palm, oak and pine,
To the forest triad divine
  To the pine, palm and oak,
    That sprang skyward and grand,
  When the morning light broke
    On the new risen land!
Each leading in order sublime,
  His own troop, innumerable, in every clime!
  Mother Earth's beauty and bloom!
    Rainbow hues and diamond dews,
    After every night's gloom;
    Pure blue sky, and wings on high,
Welcoming life from the billowy sea.
  From the sea foam then
  Came the mother of men,
And we humans had leave to be.
  Thanks to the leaves that drank
  The deadly odors rank,
    And turned them into wood.
  Thanks to the cooling shades
  That gemmed the verdant glades,
    Shedding fragrance, joy and food.
Hark! east and west, sounds in the air appalling!
Don't you hear the cedars of Lebanon calling —
" Men will fall, if too many trees are falling!"
Don't you hear the voice of Yosemite —
"If forests perish, men will come to the same extremity."
  Shall we who dig from mines
    The forests of primeval ages
  For warmth, and light to read the lines
    Of Hood's and Bryant's deathless pages,
  Prove ingrates; strip the hills of pines;
Trample, like idiots, on the fore germs,
And sink ourselves in fact, to canker-worms.

FORESTS.

The civilization of the human race naturally makes war upon the forests. That race is dominant, progressive, more and more subjecting to its control all the rest of the world — mineral, vegetable and animal. But this victory may be overdone, so as to end in inglorious defeat. The enemies of man are numberless; so are his friends. The struggle for supremacy must regard both. There can be no abiding victory over the former, without alliance with the latter. The forces of nature have habits, or self-existing laws, which cannot be safely ignored, trifled with, or reversed, whoever may attempt it.

Vitality is divided into two great departments, the stationary and the locomotive — vegetable and animal — life. Under the eternal, incomprehensible forces of nature, they started together, with ruder forms than we now see, and one necessarily complementary to the other.

In the paleozoic times immense treasures of vital force were sandwiched between the rocks, the product, probably, of both vegetable and animal life — immense forests, overwhelmed on land, alternating with the whales of dried up seas — to be used by the ingenious men of these cenozoic times, in the shape of coal or petroleum. But these treasures are not absolutely inexhaustible. The consumption of hundreds and thousands of millions of tons a year must make an end of them at last. But this is not the whole or the worst of the danger. The oxydation of these vast quantities of carbon, and hydro carbons, will lead back to a state of the atmosphere in which only the coarsest of locomotive monsters can breathe or maintain animal life. Let the men who have set up the iron-horse and spider-webbed the continents with iron roads tell us how they expect to deoxydize the poisonous carbonic acid they set afloat, *if they destroy the forests of the present day — indeed, if they do not increase their deoxydizing power many times.* Let the capitalists who have built tall chimneys beside the streams that formerly drove their busy mills, in pure air, tell us how their multitude of operatives are to breathe, if they don't have a pine forest somewhere to drink up the poison of every chimney. Indeed, how are they to breathe themselves, unless they can have the teeming, working population hale and happy? By the time the coal is all burned up, if the forests do not prevent it, the flood of carbonic acid, even on the mountain tops, will be worse than Noah's flood of water, and no ark to save anybody.

The millions of human beings in a vast city, if there were no forests in the back country, would perish in the chokedamp produced by their own lungs. More or less, they are always perishing from that very cause. Great, air-purifying forests are as necessary to every city as its water supply, and need not cost one-tenth as much. How long will it take to arouse the thinking, well-educated population of the most enlightened city to the importance of this thoroughly demonstrated fact? Must we send them back to their school books — to their first lessons in chemistry and botany? Have they forgotten all they learned in high school or college? Is that money wasted? Of what use is money handed down to posterity, if that posterity will have to breathe poisoned air all its life? A few dollars now will turn the tide in favor of forest culture, and in less than a hundred years the puny, scrubby growth of our thousands of rocky hills will give place to lofty pines, capable of purifying the air, let our industrious descendants run all the furnaces they please. The healing fragrance of those forests will plant roses on cheeks where nothing else would grow but lilies. This argument, it is to be hoped, will not be lost on the well-schooled women of Massachusetts, and surely not upon the college-bred men.

One step in the right direction has been taken. The General Court of Massachusetts has given to every city and town the right to devote land to forest culture — the title vesting in the State, and the land to be under the care of a State board — on the same terms as land can be taken for streets or roads. The city government can act for the city, and two-thirds of the voters in any regularly called town meeting for the town.

Not many cities possess territory adequate for the purpose, to be devoted to forestry. But their wealth, collectively or individually, can help neighboring towns to do it, and for this the law provides.

The cluster of cities of which Boston is the largest, and which are practically a unit, has no space for a considerable forest within it, but excellent sites within ten miles from the centre on every side. Among these, the most advantageous, because the question of water supply is involved in it, is the Middlesex Fells.

It is a tract of about 4,000 acres, including the water, a very small part of which ever has been or ever can be devoted to anything else than forest growth. But the forest there has not had fair play. The axes and the fires of civilization have changed most of it from lofty growths of white pine and hemlock to tangled thickets of scrub oaks and briers. It is just the spot of all Massachusetts to test the experiment of applying the new science of forestry, so ably cultivated by Harvard University on the Bussey farm, to the restoration of the pine on our rockiest hills. If we succeed here, there can be no failure anywhere.

That success is perfectly sure, any person can convince himself or herself by a short ramble in almost any part of the Fells. There are spots where lofty pines or hemlocks may be seen growing on soil, or rather among rocks, no better than the rest, and where no other tree will grow to any considerable size. In other spots pine stumps may be found cut so recently as to betray the age of the tree, proving that a tree must have grown to the diameter of eighteen inches or more in fifty or sixty years, where it could get almost nothing from the earth except anchorage and moisture in the crevices of the rocks, and must have derived its food from the air. Deciduous trees may make a large growth in the valleys, if properly thinned out and guarded from fire, but the white pine is perhaps the tree best suited to the rocky hills, all of which it will naturally take possession of in time, if fire is excluded. But as it does not sprout from roots left in the ground, its growth may be very much hastened by planting, and removing the other less suitable or valuable trees which stand in its way. The superfluous or obstructive wood will pay for the labor of taking it away, and making the paths by which the forest may be traversed for health and pleasure. The process will be greatly accelerated by first conveying to the tops of the hills the muck which has for ages accumulated in the little swamps and tarns at their feet, and this in some cases is quite essential to the purity of the water supply on which most of the surrounding towns depend.

To extinguish the titles of about 150 individual proprietors will cost, probably, nearly $350,000. Considering how much the five towns in which the territory lies will be benefited by its reforesting, and that their aggregate taxable value is not less than $25,000,000, the expense seems small, even for them to bear the whole. But the cities of these Boston peninsulas will inevitably derive a benefit many times worth the cost. To expedite a matter which is sure to come in time, though at a much greater expense, it is proposed to raise a subscription, conditional on the agreement of the city of Malden and the four towns to accept the new forest law, which it is hoped will amount to such a sum as will secure substantially a unanimous vote. There is not a citizen of Massachusetts, rich or poor, who is not deeply interested to have this experiment succeed, and as expeditiously as science, labor and money can make it.

THE MIDDLESEX FELLS.

[*Boston Transcript*, Sept. 25, 1882.]

As president and treasurer of the Middlesex Fells Association, formed about two years ago, I have to say that any donation to its funds constitutes a person a member, without distinction of age, complexion or sex. The association has succeeded in obtaining from the Legislature all that it asked, and somewhat more in the act of the last session, for the preservation and reproduction of forests. Every town has now the power to take land for forests, to be paid for as if it were taken for roads or streets, the title to vest in the State, and the domain to be under the care of the State Board of Agriculture, as a Board of Forestry. The forests themselves will pay the expense. The only cost is to extinguish the individual titles. As to the four thousand acres of Middlesex Fells, this cost will not exceed $300,000, for some of the territory already belongs to the towns, and not less than $20,000 in cash and land has already been subscribed on the condition that the towns interested shall vote to accept the act in regard to the entire domain proposed.

The association has hitherto expended what little money it has received in calling public attention to the matter, and is out of debt. It will need some more money to pay for the surveys and maps necessary to bring the subject before the towns for their vote, which it proposes to raise by entertainments which will interest and enlighten the public as well. A large committee of wide-awake ladies, in Boston and Middlesex County, has charge of this matter and will be seasonably heard from.

In the meantime, I was surprised last week, at an informal gathering of men, women and children in the eastern Fells, to receive a little purse of $2.30, made up by twenty children of Melrose, who appeared with bright faces on the ground and asked to be members of the association. They had all given one or two dimes apiece, and I have their names recorded as members. This sum shall not go for the preliminary expenses, but to extinguish the individual titles, if we get the requisite votes from the towns. I have since received $15 from a Boston lady, who is warmly in favor of the trees. As treasurer of the association, I have deposited the amount, $17.30, in the Five Cent Savings Bank — where I hope it will attract other donations — till such time as it may be needed. As there are not less than half a million of people living within ten miles, who will have the enjoyment of the great pine forests of the Fells if they become a public domain, it would be nothing miraculous if all the funds needed should be raised by the small contributions of the women and children.

HELP FOR THE TREES.

[*Boston Herald*, Sept. 28, 1882.]

There is nothing more useful or beautiful than a tree. But when the wood-chopper comes along it cannot help itself. It can neither run nor resist. Before axes and saws whole forests are disappearing, leaving the hills bare and barren. The "very stones" cry out against such ruthless havoc. Our wisest statesmen are alarmed, and tell us if something is not done to prevent forest fires and reproduce the trees as fast as they are consumed, the country will soon have no timber and only occasional floods instead of rivers. History tells us of such calamities. The Kings of Babylon in the valley of the Euphrates were terrible wood-choppers. When one of them died, a sublime poet sang that the fir trees and the cedars rejoiced.

> "Since thou art laid down
> No feller has come up against us."

The forests of that empire were destroyed and the men have decayed.

Trees purify the air. Forests preserve the springs. They are the grand old heart-and-health-giving hosts of our festivals and rambles — most eloquent in the golden silence of their sunlit boughs. Science has learned, after studying thousands of years, that a forest occupying a soil unfit for the growth of cereals should never be destroyed or cut away clean, like a crop of rye. It yields most by cutting only the trees that have ceased to grow, or which obstruct the growth of better trees. By this method the most sterile soil can be made to yield as much value as the most fertile, because trees, and especially resinous ones, get their nourishment mostly from the air, taking from it whatever is poisonous to animals. This principle the Legislature of our state has embodied in the law recently passed for the preservation and reproduction of forests.

This law, by a two-thirds vote of the towns of Stoneham, Winchester, Medford and Melrose and the act of the aldermen and common council of the city of Malden, can be applied to a tract of 4,000 acres now known by the name of Middlesex Fells.

If such co-operation is had, the whole tract will become a public domain, under the care of the state board of agriculture, subject to the regulations prescribed by the law. These will not necessarily dispossess any of the present inhabitants, who will be compensated for the property taken, and become tenants of the state, if they choose to remain, on terms satisfactory to the forestry board.

All people living within 10 miles of this much abused but still beautiful region are interested in the speediest possible success of this enterprise. And this includes not only the towns and city above mentioned, but Boston, Cambridge, Somerville, Chelsea, Reading and Woburn. Nothing is wanted but to awaken the people — men, women and children — to the facts of the case. To do this some money must be raised to make known the facts. Then, to induce the necessary action of the several towns within whose jurisdiction the territory lies, it will be well to raise a large subscription of money conditional on such action, because it will probably cost about $300,000 — the assessed value — to extinguish the individual titles, and the towns will not be likely to use the right of eminent domain granted to them by the law, if they must thereby add $300,000 to their taxes; and especially when all the cities above-named will be as much benefited as themselves, for it is to belong to the state, and will serve as a state as well as a town park.

THE PUBLIC DOMAIN.

INFLUENCE OF FORESTS UPON THE CLIMATE OF A COUNTRY. THE PROJECT OF A FOREST RESORT NEAR BOSTON.—THE MIDDLESEX FELLS AND THEIR IMPORTANCE TO US.

[January, 1883.]

The civilized world is beginning to move in favor of forests, and for many good reasons. One of the strongest was referred to by Prof. Huxley some years ago, at the unveiling of the statue of Dr. Priestley, the man who discovered oxygen gas, in these words: "He laid the foundation of gas analysis; he discovered the complementary actions of animal and vegetable life upon the constituents of the atmosphere." This means that the salubrity of climate depends on the purity of the atmosphere, and the purity of the atmosphere depends largely on the action of forests. Science calls on men more and more loudly to care for trees. The ancients seem to have known intuitively that the atmosphere of forests was salubrious and health-giving, and held them in the highest estimation. The Romans and other ancient peoples greatly venerated them, temples being often erected and sacrifices ordained in their honor. This may be considered one of the greatest reasons for the Druids living in them, as it was thought much more sacred to dwell under trees than in the open field. In England the forests have long been in possession of and under protection from the crown. William the Conqueror, after the conquest, enlarged the forests, and strict laws against trespassing upon them were enacted. Under his successors vast tracts of country were depopulated in order to create new forests or to extend the limits of old ones. One of the grievances against Charles I., who lost his head, was that he took advantage of the encroachments on these public domains to extort money from persons who had extended their lands inside the forest boundaries. All, or nearly all, the English forests were very ancient. In Coke's time there were 69 royal forests, all of which, with the exception of the New forest in Hampshire, created by William the Conqueror, and Hampton Court forest, by Henry VIII., were so ancient that no record afforded any information as to their commencement. In Norway the forest land extends up to Drontheim, which is in N. lat. 63°. Switzerland is well wooded, and oaks and firs are found at a level over 4,000 feet above the sea. France has some fine examples, her variety of climate being favorable to the growth of all species of trees, some of which indeed belong to a much warmer climate; the forests of Ardennes and the Bois de Boulogne may be mentioned as instances of the expanses which have been covered with trees. In Italy the plains of Ravenna afford a wide scope for the luxuriance of forest life. The pine there grows extensively. Much of the oak used in constructing British war ships comes from Italy. Russia, however, is the most heavily wooded country of the whole world, and some of the finest timber known comes from her ports in the Baltic. The districts of Twer and Novgorod are well covered with wood, and the forest of Volkonsky is said to be the largest in Europe. Poland, too, resembles Russia in this matter, and she may be considered the second well-wooded country in the old world. North and South America were originally almost entirely covered with grand forests, and South America can still boast of vast tracts of wood-land — the whole of the valley of the Amazon, which embraces one-third of the entire area of that section of our continent, may be said to be in effect one vast forest. In North America, it is well known, the grand old forests are gradually disappearing, through the immigration of settlers from abroad, the immigration of other settlers from the older states to the new states and territories, as well as from the large lumbering industry which systematically wipes out forest after forest, until thoughtful people are becoming aroused to the dangers of such decimation and alive to the importance of, at least, encouraging the planting of new forests in all sections of the country which have become thickly settled. For about 100 years past a distinct science of forestry has been arising in Europe, with the happiest practical results, both hygienic and economical. At last it has begun to invade this continent, where hitherto the forests, as well as the men of the forests, have been looked upon as a common enemy, to be exterminated no matter how soon. All the land, whatever its quality, has been appropriated to individuals. But the life of individual men is so much shorter than that of the best species of trees, that, with extremely few exceptions, no proper care is taken of the forests, even on land fit for nothing else. The short-lived individual destroys the capital to realize a profit before he dies. But everything that breathes has an interest in forests. Hence the propriety of having public forest domains, so that a public, which does not die, may realize the highest profit by keeping up the capital. A recent European forestry report states that an oak, in its favorite soil, makes, at the age of 200 years, eight times as much wood in a year as it did at the age of 50 years. White pines will likewise grow more and more, for perhaps 100 or 200 years, on a soil where an oak will cease to grow at the age of 50, or, perhaps, 30 years — the pine deriving so much more sustenance from the air than from the soil.

It is a very creditable thing to the Legislature of Massachusetts that it last year passed, almost unanimously, an act authorizing towns and cities to appropriate, by a two-thirds vote, any land within their territory for the purpose of reproducing and preserving forests, the same to be paid for as if taken for highways. The individual titles being thus extinguished, the title is to vest in the state, and the domain is to be taken care of, the board of agriculture acting as a board of forestry. This general act was asked for by the five municipalities in which is situated the wild and rocky land recently named the Middlesex Fells. It consists of about 4,000 acres, including a natural lake of 380 acres, and artificial reservoirs of nearly 200 acres more. The rest of the surface consists of rocky ridges, ravines and tarns — bogs or marshes. Spot Pond is elevated 170 feet above tidewater, and the two artificial reservoirs, which supply Winchester with water, are nearly on the same level. A good many of the hills rise from 50 to 100 feet higher, and command fine views of Boston, its harbor and neighboring towns and cities. The population is exceedingly sparse. Most of the tract consists of wood lots belonging to non-residents, of whom there are considerably more than 100. The whole of the real estate valuation for taxes cannot exceed $300,000. Most of the wood lots have been desolated by the wood-choppers within the past 30 years. So little care is taken of the young trees, that fire every year is allowed to destroy more than half the profit of a forest growth. All the hills were once covered with white pine, hemlock and cedar, of which only a few patches are now left — but they are exceedingly beautiful. The whole tract lies between the six and nine-mile circles, of which Boston City Hall is the centre, and thus offers to the city of Boston the grandest forest park to be found near a large city in any part of the world. A year or two of such a resort would save its cost in doctors' bills to the people of this city, to say nothing of its value to the municipalities that include it in preserving their water supply. In a very few years, if not made a public domain, it will be covered with villages, the filth from which must inevitably drain into the lake and reservoirs which now take up no inconsiderable portion of its surface. The whole people, rich and poor, will soon be called to help, according to their ability, in the application to the Middlesex Fells of the law above referred to. Once the individual titles are extinguished, success will surely crown an experiment which will be followed throughout this and other states.

A PLEA FOR THE FELLS.
[Jan. 9, 1883.]

The trees have voices. The forest is a grand symphony. The buds, blossoms and leaves inspire musicians, painters and poets. Every spring there is a resurrection of the chorus. Every autumn there is the grand finale and requiem. The mighty pines, defying the storms, crown the hills and say, "Never mind the pale snows. Summer will come again. Sleep in your bark, gentle sisters; June will bring out your broad leaves, and we shall all be gay."

Do the men and women who glory in art not know that Nature is the mother of Art? Will they coddle the daughter and let the mother perish among thieves and murderers? Only shams will do that!

THE MIDDLESEX FELLS.
[*Boston Transcript*, Jan. 26, 1883.]

As nearly as can be ascertained from the tax lists, the real estate in the four thousand acres of the territory which is proposed to be made a "public domain" has been valued for taxation at not more than $300,000. This is undoubtedly above its real value, because the assessments were generally made when there was much more wood standing, and have seldom been reduced since; and the above sum includes about five hundred acres which is now town property. The buildings are worth about $60,000, and, after the individual titles are extinguished, most of them may be rented for purposes not inconsistent with the preservation and reproduction of the forest. There will be no necessity of a general eviction. Thus a revenue of three or four thousand dollars a year will accrue — at least sufficient to pay for preventing fires.

The creation of a public forest around their water supply will be of immense benefit to four of the municipalities that are called upon to cede territory. Ordinary prudence would and must lead them to cede their territory, cost what it may, in money and loss of taxable basis, provided Stoneham, which contains most of the water, but does not use a drop, should cede its part. But if the four municipalities concerned in the water supply were to cede their territory, and Stoneham not to cede that which is required from her, there would, in a very few years, be a large village draining inevitably into Spot Pond, which would make its water unfit to drink. Hence all five of the municipalities must act concurrently or not at all.

The question with Stoneham will be whether it can afford to give up nearly five per cent. of its taxable basis of real estate for the advantage it will receive from the public domain. Certainly there will be an immediate sacrifice. But it is equally certain that there will be an ultimate gain. In a very few years, if not in one, the residual territory of Stoneham will be worth more than the whole is now. A village, with three miles of very attractive pine forest between it and Boston, growing more and more beautiful every year, will not have to wait more than ten years to see its population and its value more than doubled. But with three miles of barren rocks, adorned with wretched shanties and tethered goats, between it and the metropolis, Stoneham will not keep pace with villages much farther off. Her thrifty mechanics and manufacturers have to choose between the two future conditions of the Middlesex Fells above described. Stoneham could afford to *give* the whole of the territory desired of her, buildings and all, and Boston many millions, to have the glorious pine forest on which Governor Winthrop looked down in 1631 restored to-day. And the intelligent and patriotic citizens of Boston are willing to pay Stoneham, as I think, the full market value of its territory in the Fells, for the chance of having the forest restored under the new law.

THE MIDDLESEX FELLS.

[*Melrose Journal*, March 17, 1883.]

I am often asked, both here and in New York, how are the "Fells" getting on? Everybody seems to be enthusiastically in favor of having the thing done — at the expense of somebody else. To have a nice pine forest of four thousand acres, within a nickel ride of Boston City Hall, would be a valuable thing for men, women, children and birds. The rocky land is there and will be, but the trees grow less every year. All the legislation has been done that need be. It only remains for the city of Malden and the four towns of Stoneham, Melrose, Medford and Winchester by concurrent vote to decree that the land within the jurisdiction of each shall be ceded to the State for the purpose expressed in chapter 255 of the Acts of 1882 and the thing is done. The law provides for the proper care of the forest and its proper enjoyment by the public. The individual owners, so far as they do not donate the land, will have to be paid for it, as if it were taken for roads. It is not likely that the towns will tax themselves in the aggregate some $300,000, which is the assessed value of the tract, including buildings, unless they have help by way of donations, though those which depend on it for water supply could better afford to do so than to have it settled with villages of shanties and goats, which is its fate in the natural course of things.

For the purpose of encouraging the five municipalities concerned to take advantage of the law above referred to, a Board of Trustees has been enlisted to hold individual obligations to aid the towns in extinguishing the present titles to the land, payable only when a majority of the said trustees is satisfied that all the desirable territory is included in the concurrent vote. These obligations are to be placed in the hands of Mr. Henry Brooks, Secretary of the Trustees, 97 Beacon street, Boston. By applying to him, or to myself, 87 Milk street (Post Office Box 109), Boston, blank forms of the conditional obligation, with the law annexed, may be obtained. Not a dollar will be required till the "Public Domain" becomes a fact. Then the obligation will be as collectible as notes in bank. There will be no begging. The people must move and act spontaneously, if anything is done. It is everybody's axe, and if everybody grinds it, it will be dull for the generations to come. The wood-choppers are sure to grind theirs while a tree is left. Here is work for the press, the pulpit, the platform — for every one that likes to breathe pure air, drink pure water and see green things. The following are all the "conditional obligations" thus far received by the Secretary:

LIST OF "CONDITIONAL OBLIGATIONS."

Elisha S. Converse, Malden	$5,000
Elizur Wright, Medford	5,000
Francis Brooks, Medford	2,260
P. C. Brooks, Medford	500
Sheperd Brooks, Medford	500
Walter C. Wright, Medford	100
Annie Wigglesworth, Boston	200
Lyman Dyke, Stoneham	125
Mary Anne Wales, Boston	100
Fenno Tudor, Nahant	100
J. Randolph Coolidge, Boston	100
A. J. Wright, Boston	25
Sarah Russell	50
Abby W. May, Boston	25
William Winsor, Philadelphia	5
Henry Winsor, Boston	5
Chas. W. Story, Brookline	2
Mary E. Liliquest, Boston	5
	$14,102

The sum of $7,385, included in the above, is the assessed value of land donated within the Fells by three individuals. This land undoubtedly cost more and is worth less than what it is assessed for.

THE VOICE OF A TREE FROM THE MIDDLESEX FELLS.

[*Boston Transcript*, Oct. 10, 1883.]

The sun unlocks the frozen sod,
And sets the rivers free:
And lo, half way from man to God,
Stands worshipping the tree.

I, who now address you, am a tree. I want your friendship. I want it for your sake as well as mine. I do not speak for myself only, but for all my kind, to your kind, for the vegetable world to the animal world. Let us henceforth be true friends, for such we naturally are. You all have the advantage of us trees, in that you move about, have teeth, axes and saws. Use them, but not to your own hurt.

Do you ask who I am? Well, I come of a good family. If my ancestors did not teach yours how to make that glory of mankind, the *wheel*, they probably did teach them to put spokes in it. The botanists call me *Pinus Strobus*, because they prefer Greek to English. I am, in plain English, the *wheel pine*, because, as I grow up towards the sky, every foot or two I shoot out five spokes, or lateral branches, and these branches keep doing the same, or nearly the same, as they start off horizontally, and then curve upward. You will know my particular family from all the other pine families by our strong predilection for the number *five*. Our perpendicular leader has not always, but almost always, exactly five spokes in his wheel. His followers may have fewer, but always five if they can. Between the youngest hubs, both the leaders and the followers put forth budlets, or leaf buds, each producing exactly five leaves, or green needles. These budlets are so disposed around the stem, spirally, that if you sever the stem above and below any consecutive five, the five groups, or five needles each, will shoot into the air in five different directions, generally seventy-two degrees apart. This is a wonderfully good arrangement for catching all the particles of tree-food floating in the air — something like that of a whale's mouth, by which that huge animal is said to live on minute animals floating in the water. This arrangement accounts for my family's wonderful tenacity of life. Wherever our roots can grapple a foothold among the New England rocks, as well as in her plains of sterile sand, we flourish in perennial green, breathe balsam into the lungs of the sick, make strong men stronger, hoard up pure springs for the thirsty, defy drought, even beyond all other trees, defy everything but fire, and will you not do your best to defend us from that? Our very blood is combustible, while that of many other trees is not. Hence, sometimes, in spite of ourselves, we destroy the human dwellings built out of our own bodies.

Let me just whisper in your ear, my kind friend, that what is our food is your poison. Don't take that on my authority. Go to your chemist, ask him what would be the effect of clapping a bell-glass over Boston. He will probably tell you that trees on the Common and Public Garden would do something toward keeping the human inhabitants from smothering in the poisonous gas of their own breath; but they not being able to consume their favorite food as fast as produced by 250,000 people (not to speak of horses and furnaces), the people and their horses, cats and dogs would soon choke and die. Without the bell-glass the winds waft away the poisonous gas which feeds the forests. Where does it go to? Why does it not come back again to plague you? What becomes of it? Ask your botanists, your chemists, all the people who have been studying the nature of things since Joseph Priestley discovered what air is made of 109 years ago. See if they will not tell you that animals could never have lived and cannot live long on this earth without forests to purify the air. You may ask the historians, too, if great nations have not decayed and become puny and degraded because they made broad and fertile valleys bare of forests.

Do you say, "What is that to me? I shall be dust long

before my country is a desert?" Perhaps I am but a living blockhead, but I hope you are something more than living dust. I hope you do not despise your own posterity, or if you neither have nor hope for any, that you have a kind regard for the posterity of your brothers and sisters, for the multitudes of conscious, thinking beings who will inhabit Boston and its surroundings a hundred years hence. Have you really such a thing in you as a human heart? That is the great question which I, a tree, the hearty friend of New England and all mankind, speaking, summer and winter, to every sense and every spark of reason you have, ask you to decide *practically*. Of course you will do it in one way or the other.

Egypt is famous for its pyramids; India for its temples, above and below ground; Europe for its vast cathedrals. They all cost incalculable human labor. They may be wonderful, beautiful, objects for the human race to be proud of. But pride, they say, precedes a fall. Would not the same amount of labor devoted to the preservation and production of trees and forests in the right places have clothed deserts in green, and made the planet better worth living in for man, woman, and child? You say, "Trees do not feel. They are not conscious of any wrong done them." But how do you know *that?* How do you *know* that? Have you ever been a tree yourself? And if you *do* know it, what difference does it make in regard to your obligation to us? Do you say, "My voice, my aid, among 50,000,000, is nothing? I don't own a tree or a place to plant one. Let the rich, let the Government take care of the forests?" Who owns the air? Who owns the Government? Would you not rather tax yourselves than have the Government tax you? Let us have your heart anyhow; and as much or little out of your purse as your head and heart, after full and fair conference, agree that you can spare, provided any plan for our and your benefit is made sure to go.

As a tree, not capable of any political or party prejudice, thankful for all the forty or hundred acre parks and gardens which the people of Boston have or are to have, let me say to you, without sarcasm or reproach, that these are not forests or substitutes for forests. A forest should be at least one hundred times as large. It should be a place where trees of all sorts adapted to the locality, once started, shall grow as thick as they can stand, till each arrives at its full maturity; and not one shall be removed till, from crowding or age, it has ceased to grow. It takes a forest of my own particular family about one hundred years to come to perfection, and in the meantime it will yield surplus wood and lumber enough to pay for taking care of it. And while it will grow faster than any other wood on a million of acres of Massachusetts land where no edible crop will grow, when it comes to perfection it will yield more value, with less labor every year, and without any diminution of its capital stock, than the best million acres of arable land. No such result is possible if a young forest is swept off, principal and interest, every twenty or thirty years. If you do not believe it, ask the foresters of Europe.

Well, it has been proposed, in behalf of a little clump or two of my brethren, left forlorn in what is called the Middlesex Fells, in which are situated the water supplies of Melrose, Malden, Medford and Winchester, and over which Stoneham looks down, proud of Cheese Rock, to extinguish all individual titles to about four thousand acres, perhaps the largest body of waste land lying compact together in the State, and vest the title in the State itself, to be taken care of by the State Board of Agriculture as a board of forestry. All the needful legislation on the part of the State is already on the statute-book. All that is needed is concurrent two-thirds votes of the five municipalities in which the territory lies. Individual proprietors who do not give their soil, or rather trees and rocks, to the State, will receive compensation, as they would for land taken for roads, from those municipalities. Not one of these municipalities can afford *not* to give its share of the territory to the State, for the purpose defined in the law, and the city of Malden would be a gainer, even if it had to assume the whole expense. But this would not be exactly just and fair, seeing that the success of the experiment of making a 4,000 acre pine forest within six miles of Boston would benefit the city and the State at least fifty times its cost. The cost of doing it in the most effective style will be less than $500,000. It will then be in a shape to pay its own way, by rents and trimmings. It will have its tree-planters and care-takers properly distributed. It will have a watch tower in the centre, from which a watchman can see the first smoke of a forest fire. In the same minute he will telephone to the care-taker nearest, who will with a green bush or a sprinkling-pot extinguish that fire in the next very few minutes. A fire that shall burn over half an acre will be impossible. This terribly dry year hundreds of acres have been burned over, doing woful damage, where any was possible. In two or three years all the rocky hills will be covered with the seedlings of my hardy and hopeful family, and the dells will glow with maples. We shall be proud of Massachusetts as soon as we know we are on her "public domain." And in ten years she, and especially Boston, will be proud of us.

If you do not believe all this, call on Mr. Francis Brooks, of 97 Beacon Street, Boston, or write to him for a copy of the "Conditional Obligation" and the late "Forest Law." The question is, How much are you willing to give towards the expense, provided that law is carried into effect?

Yours truly,
PINUS STROBUS.

THE NEW FORESTRY LAW.

[CHAP. 255, ACTS OF 1882.]

AN ACT authorizing towns and cities to provide for the preservation and reproduction of Forests.

Be it enacted, etc., as follows :

SECTION 1. The voters of any town, at a meeting legally called for the purpose, and the city council of any city, may, for the purpose of devoting a portion of the territory of such town or city to the preservation, reproduction and culture of forest trees for the sake of the wood and timber thereon, or for the preservation of the water supply of such town or city, take or purchase any land within the limits of such town or city, may make appropriations of money for such taking or purchase, may receive donations of money or land for the said purposes, and may make a public domain of the land so devoted, subject to the regulations hereinafter prescribed. The title of all lands so taken, purchased or received shall vest in the Commonwealth, and shall be held in perpetuity for the benefit of the town or city in which such land is situated.

SECT. 2. A town or city taking land shall, within sixty days after such taking, file and cause to be recorded in the registry of deeds for the county or district in which the land is situated a description thereof sufficiently accurate for identifying the same. In case such town or city and the owner of such land do not agree upon the damage occasioned by such taking, such damage shall be ascertained and determined in the manner provided in case of the taking of land for a highway in such town or city, and such town or city shall thereupon pay such sums as may finally be determined to be due.

SECT. 3. The state board of agriculture shall act as a BOARD OF FORESTRY, without pay, except for necessary travelling expenses, and shall have the supervision and management of all such public domains, and shall make all necessary regulations for their care and use and for the increase and preservation of the timber wood and undergrowth thereon, and for the planting and cultivating of trees therein. The said board shall appoint one or more persons, to be called KEEPERS, to have charge, subject to its direction, of each such public domain, enforce its regulations and perform such labor thereon as said board shall require; and said keepers shall have the same power to protect such domain from injury and trespass, and to keep the peace therein as constables and police officers in towns.

SECT. 4. Said board may lease any building that may be on any such public domain on such terms as it shall deem expedient. All sums which may be derived from rents and from the sale of the products of any such domain shall be paid to said board and shall be applied by it, so far as necessary, to the management, care, cultivation and improvement of such domain; and any surplus remaining in any year shall be paid over to the city or town in which such domain is situated. Said board shall not, however, expend upon or on account of such public domain in any year a greater amount than it receives as aforesaid.

SECT. 5. A city or town in which any such public domain is situated may erect thereon any building for public instruction or recreation, provided that such use thereof is not in the judgment of said board inconsistent with the purposes expressed in section one.

SECT. 6. No land shall be taken or purchased, no building shall be erected on any such domain, and no expenditures shall be authorized or made, or liability be incurred under this act by any city or town until an appropriation sufficient to cover the estimated expense thereof shall in a town have been made by a vote of TWO-THIRDS of the legal voters of such town present and voting in a legal town meeting called for the purpose, or in a city by a vote of two-thirds of each branch of the city council of such city; such expenditures shall in no case exceed the appropriations made therefor, and all contracts made for expenditures beyond the amount of such appropriations shall be void ; and all expenditures under this act shall be subject to the laws of this Commonwealth limiting municipal indebtedness.

SECT. 7. For the purpose of defraying the expenses incurred under the provisions of this act, any town or the city council of any city may issue from time to time, and to an amount not exceeding the sum actually expended for the taking or purchase of lands for such public domain, bonds or certificates of debt, to be denominated on the face thereof the "Public Domain Loan," and to bear interest at such rates, and to be payable at such times as such town or city council may determine ; and for the redemption of such loan such town or city council shall establish a sinking fund, sufficient, with accumulating interest, to provide for the payment of such loan at maturity. All amounts received on account of such public domain shall be paid into such sinking fund until such fund shall amount to a sum sufficient, with its accumulations, to pay at maturity the bonds for the security of which the fund was established.

SECT. 8. This act shall take effect upon its passage.
[*Approved May* 25, 1882.]

A considerable number of OBLIGATIONS, of the following form, for sums ranging from $2 to $5,000, have already been signed, and are in the hands of Mr. FRANCIS BROOKS, one of the TRUSTEES. It is very desirable that he should have, before the next March town-meetings, a sufficient amount to make the concurrent votes certain. Till favorable votes of all the five municipalities are obtained, no payment can be called for. And when any obligation is cancelled by payment, it will be to the obligor a valuable and honorable historical document to hand down to his or her posterity.

FORM OF CONDITIONAL OBLIGATION.

PUBLIC DOMAIN.

I,..,
of ....,
do hereby promise, on the conditions hereinafter stated, to pay to ELISHA S. CONVERSE, SAMUEL E. SEWALL, JOHN D. LONG, BENJAMIN

F. BUTLER, ALBERT PALMER, EDMUND DWIGHT, FRANCIS BROOKS, GEORGE E. ROGERS, FRANK B. FAY, LYMAN DIKE, DANIEL NEEDHAM, JOSEPH D. WILDE, ELIZUR WRIGHT, Mrs. GEORGE L. STEARNS, Mrs. JULIA WARD HOWE, Mrs. Dr. I. T. TALBOT, Miss ABBY MAY, Mrs. M. HEMENWAY, Mrs. JOHN E. LODGE, Mrs. EX-GOVERNOR CLAFLIN, T. W. HIGGINSON, HENRY BROOKS, Mrs. MARY A. LIVERMORE, Mrs. LUTHER HILL, Mrs. PROFESSOR C. E. PICKERING, Mrs. CHARLES SPRAGUE, *Trustees*, the sum of..Dollars, as a donation for the purpose of setting apart and establishing a certain tract of land, called the Middlesex Fells, as a Public Domain, under Chapter 255 of the Acts of 1882, hereunto annexed; such sum of ....Dollars to be paid by me on demand of a majority of said Trustees, either in cash or by deed of land within the said domain, at its assessed value for taxation, whenever the towns of Stoneham, Medford, Winchester, Melrose, and the city of Malden, each and all of them, by vote or resolution, according to said Act, shall have taken such land, appropriating for the same such sums as a majority of said Trustees shall deem reasonable, and within such boundaries as shall be satisfactory to them; it being understood that — and it is one of the conditions of this obligation — the funds coming into the hands of the said Trustees shall be paid to the several towns in proportion to the assessed value of the real estate to be paid for by each; and that any excess remaining in their hands after all the individual titles are extinguished shall be expended, under their direction, with the consent of the Board of Agriculture acting as a "Board of Forestry," in making roads and paths for the convenience and pleasure of the public.

Signed :

Witness :

THE FUNCTION OF FORESTS.

A PAPER READ BEFORE THE APPALACHIAN MOUNTAIN CLUB
JAN. 9, 1884.

To this mountaineer club, in which I am but a neophyte, I can give no details not already known to every one of you. But I highly prize the privilege of making some general observations on the relation of trees to animals, and more particularly on the relation of forests to the human population of this continent. The health of the forests is the health of the people. Our nation, after slumbering 100 years, while the axe has been going on to make the continent look like a clipped horse with only the mane and tail in a natural state, is beginning to open its eyes. The reason of the profound sleep is, that, till a very little while ago, nobody knew what air, water and earth were made of, how trees grew, or whether their growth had any relation to animal life or not. You all know and honor the great practical philosopher who "tore from the sky the thunderbolt and the sceptre from tyrants" (Eripuit cœlo fulmen sceptrumque tyrannis). He was a Boston boy. His bosom friend was one Joseph Priestley, a Unitarian minister of Birmingham, Eng. Some nine or ten years ago, on the occasion of unveiling a statue of this Joseph Priestley in Birmingham, the celebrated scientist, Prof. Huxley said: "Priestley laid the foundation of gas analysis; he discovered the complementary actions of animal and vegetable life upon the constituents of the atmosphere; and, finally, he crowned his work, this day 100 years ago, by the discovery of that 'pure dephlogisticated air,' to which the French chemists subsequently gave the name of oxygen."

From this sublime, this supereminently vital, discovery, there has resulted a considerably general knowledge of the fact that what is poison to the breathing animal is food for the vegetable — that the tree, by purifying the air, is the most important friend of man.

One of the oldest books says: "The tree of the field is man's life," (Deuteronomy xx., 19,) and this is true of every tree of the forest. But it often takes more than 100 years after a discovery to develop a practical utility. To warm-blooded, breathing animals, the most dangerous poison is the gas once called carbonic acid, or more recently carbon deutoxide. This deadly gas is constantly pouring into the atmosphere from at least four abundant sources: 1. From the lungs of all breathing animals. 2. From the natural decomposition of both animals and vegetables. 3. From all fires and furnaces. 4. From all volcanoes, active or quiescent.

Now what saves the human race, or is to save it, in these days, when not only lungs are multiplied, but furnaces, for gas, locomotives, not to speak of volcanoes, from smothering in an atmosphere of choke damp? Let Prof. Balfour, perhaps the highest botanical authority in the world, answer: "The function of respiration in animals consists in the giving out of carbonic acid, or, in other words, the oxidation of carbon, while the great function of vegetables is the elimination of oxygen, or the deoxidation of carbonic acid. The two processes are antagonistic, and a balance is kept up between the carbonic acid given off by animals, etc., and the oxygen given out by plants. A grown person is said to give off $3\frac{1}{2}$ pounds of carbon in a day, and every pound of carbon burnt or oxidized yields more than $3\frac{1}{2}$ pounds of carbonic acid."

I think if the professor had been as much of a chemist as a botanist he would have said every pound of carbon burnt or oxidized would make exactly three pounds of carbonic acid. But his blunder as a chemist does not hurt his authority as a botanist. For $3\frac{1}{2}$ pounds of carbon burnt certainly makes $10\frac{1}{2}$ pounds of carbonic acid, and that, at the ordinary atmospheric pressure, will fill something over 110 cubic feet of space. As it takes but a small percentage of carbonic acid, mixed with pure air, to make it irrespirable, it is easy to see how a crowded assembly in an ill-ventilated room poisons itself. As carbonic acid is a gas half as heavy again as pure air, it inclines to take the lowest place. It settles in wells, cellars, caves, valleys. Its tendencies are not Appalachian. Yet, being at all ordinary temperatures a gas, the air currents are always lifting it up to feed the trees on hills and at the bases of the mountain summits. Plainly, but for the forests, the chief, if not the only consumers, man, if not all other animals, at no very distant day would cease to exist. The great cities, usually not much above sea level, would stifle in the poisonous gas. Even Quito might perish for lack of oxygen. The functions of man and trees, says Prof. Balfour, are "antagonistic." This seems hardly the word. I would rather say they are interdependent, or complementary. In truth, as we may well suspect from history, as geologically recorded, the trees came first. They were the forerunners, the John Baptists, who prepared the way for men and women, by purifying the air from the poisonous carbonic acid. They not only made the air respirable for the deinotherum, but they laid up between the leaves of Mother Terra's vast book stores of coal for the use of the smelting and cooking animal to be developed after countless centuries.

Now, ladies and gentlemen of a club that knows the value of pure oxygen, properly diluted with pure nitrogen, by actual experience, is it too soon for men and women to establish a hearty, practical appreciation of the hygienic dependence of our race on the forests? Shall we not restore to all the hilltops of our beloved Massachusetts the glorious pines that breathed balsams summer and winter on our brave ancestors 200 years ago?

It is often said, to allay apprehension and promote slumber on this subject, that there is now more woodland in Massachusetts than there was 40 years ago. I think it is true. At any rate there is more bush pasture. But barberry bushes and scrub oaks are not forests. If the bush pastures are ever converted into forests, it will be through the wisely directed labors of people who can distinguish between trees, and put the right seeds in the right places. Massachusetts has fit places for every tree that is anywhere at home in this latitude, but the proper tree for her rugged, rocky hills is the glorious white pine. A pine seed hardly needs more than a peck of dirt on a bare rock to erect upon it in 30 or 40 years a tower of perennial green as high as a church steeple. Cover the hills with pine, and then oaks, maples, white ash and black walnuts will rejoice in the ravines and valleys. Let us promote forests and we shall save the streams. Gelid fountains and purling brooks can only gladden our trying summers by having large forests on the high lands to screen the surface from the pitiless sun. Let the axe convert the forests into scrubs and all the hills be scorched and the grass will wither on the plains and in the valleys.

The most odious of all diseases to the human animal are the skin diseases. The human leper has always been intolerable. What leprosy is to the individual mortal, such is the utter destruction of the forests to our general mother earth. Are men and women to prove themselves more pestilent parasites on the face of nature, converting this glorious planet into an abode of life more miserable than death itself? What is our civilization good for, if it cannot preserve and increase the conditions of the highest possible health for the human race and its auxiliary animals?

THE PUBLIC DOMAIN.

THE ATMOSPHERE OF HEAVEN THE ATMOSPHERE OF THE PEOPLE.

[*Boston Herald*, May 30, 1884.]

The year 1882 produced a law in Massachusetts, chap. 255, which a competent authority has pronounced the wisest placed on her statute books for 50 years. It proposes for the people a common interest in all such land as cannot be profitably managed by individuals. Such is the case with about one-quarter of the surface of our mountainous Massachusetts. As individual property, it is of little value, because wood is the only crop it can grow, and the life of the individual owner, provided he had the requisite knowledge, is too short for him to wait for the maximum annual production of a forest before taking his harvest. Forestry must be the function of the government; only agriculture or gardening of the individual.

Henry George is right enough as to the rocky hills and gorges of New England. With a little labor and care, under scientific foresters, they might be made, in less than a hundred years, to supply other states, as well as themselves, with white pine, maple, oak and ash, and pay all our taxes. No farmer would be the poorer. All would breathe purer air. Fewer would perish by lung poison. But as to the government owning all the corn, potato, meadow and orchard land, and mankind being tenants of the government, Mr. George dreams. Let us first try the government as landlord on the forest — on land that cannot possibly be made worse than it is. Even bad governments have saved the forests of Europe to some extent. Should life become more intolerable under a good government than it is even in Spain for want of forests?

I am writing this to remind every man, woman and child in Massachusetts of his or her interest in the question of making the 4,000 acres of the Middlesex Fells a public domain, under the act of 1882. The atmosphere of this earth is your atmosphere. You own it as much as the millionaires do. You have more reason than they to look out for its purity near home, for few of you can flit off, as they can, 500 or 1,000 miles whenever you get out of breath. You want a great piney wood, where you can get an hour's snuffing of fresh, balsamic air for a dime or two. Let me invite you all to attend to your own interests in regard to the Middlesex Fells. Come out there, especially on that great, patriotic day, the Seventeenth of June — Tuesday, this year — or, if it storms, the next fair day. See the miracle of the green leaves on every bush. See how nature can raise enormous white pines where no other tree can grow.

If the people of Boston, Charlestown, Chelsea, Somerville and Cambridge, to say nothing of the municipalities of Malden, Medford, Winchester, Stoneham and Melrose, where the territory lies, only knew the value to them of making that 4,000 acres a public domain, for the purposes stated in the law, not another year would pass before the thing would be accomplished. That fact would revolutionize the forestry of Massachusetts. It would secure to Boston's posterity the loveliest forest park on this or any continent.

It is hoped that all persons, women as well as men, interested in the law above referred to, will call at my office, New England Life building, Postoffice square, and obtain copies of the law for general circulation, and likewise attend a meeting on the top of Pine hill, Medford, June 17, at 3 P.M., there, if possible, to reorganize the Middlesex Fells Association with force enough to carry through a project which enlisted the enthusiasm of such departed worthies as William Foster Eaton, John Owen and Wilson Flagg.

103

THE PUBLIC DOMAIN.

[*Boston Transcript*, June 9, 1884.]

There is a tract in Middlesex County, large enough for a township, taking up about half of two and overlapping into three others, which Nature has doomed to be either the disgrace or the crowning ornament of our Massachusetts civilization.

In geological terms, it was the volcanic centre of the Laurentian upheaval of this country some time ago. Then the ice age came on, put the fires out, ground off the ragged edges of the rocks, and left the crater a pond on a hill. Some soil was left in the ravines. The trees, especially the white pines, took possession, concealing all the rocks both summer and winter. Then came our ancestors, with more thrift than geology. Their axes and saw mills soon revealed the rocks. So they divided the land into at least one hundred forty-acre farms, with abundance of stone walls. Three or four of these farms were worth the walls. The rest became hard scrabble wood lots — brush pastures for rabbits, partridges and woodchucks. Frequent fires keep the pines few.

Yet in the early years of this century, William Foster who, in his military career in France, had been smitten with the beauty of the French chateaux, in wild and rocky places, built his summer residence on the eastern shore of Spot Pond, ineffectually christened by him Lake Wyoming. He labored, almost in vain, to inspire Bostonians with the superlative beauty of the scenery in his neighborhood. At last in despair of attracting settlers of taste worthy the locality, he gave to the Franklin Institute most of his land, which allowed it to be sold for taxes. The late Mr. Eaton, who owned the beautiful chateau next to Mr. Foster's and would have given the city of Boston $100,000 toward a park embracing the Fells, was obliged to dispose of his wealth otherwise.

Boston was not sensible of the situation. Its eyes seemed to be in the back of its head. It saw the "Old South," the darling "old lion and the unicorn," but it did not see its future self, embosoming a delectable evergreen forest, watered with pure lakes, where a dime would give every sick child the chance to breathe the purest possible air,— where in every summer holiday, or other day, a hundred social picnics could be enjoyed, without interfering with each other.

The Middlesex Fells as a great pine forest — a Bois des Rochers — in the centre of Boston, is a dream of the future not wilder than a good deal of the past. Before you so stigmatize it, please take a look.

Begin with Stoneham village. You know all about Dorchester, Roxbury, Brookline and Brighton. Cambridge, Somerville, Chelsea, are themselves cities, but in reality as much Boston as some of the former. Then there are Wilmington, Malden and Melrose, very much Bostonian. Stoneham is hid behind the rocks and the scrub oaks of the vast Fells. Yet Stoneham for grandeur and beauty of situation, is above all the places I have mentioned. It is high up in the pure air — purified from the smoke and smother of the city by the intervening Fells.

It cannot enjoy Spot Pond, wholly in its own territory, without a pump. If it will vote for the "public domain," the land it will have left will become the most fashionable and valuable part of Boston as soon as the children just born are ready to keep house.

The "public domain" wants only a little encouragement. It has all the law that is needed. Everybody thinks it will benefit everybody, and that some rich person or other will certainly buy it and give it to the State. How much grander it would be if three hundred thousand fathers and mothers, whose children are to enjoy it, would promise a dollar each towards extinguishing the individual titles, and thus encourage the municipalities to vote the cession of the territory to the State. All that is wanted is the spontaneous public spirit which would surely kindle into a blaze if the people of Boston would make up a score of picnics in the Fells on this next seventeenth. I don't think that any proprietor of a wood lot would object to their use of his premises, if they are careful not to set the dry leaves on fire.

They shall be welcome to any grove of mine, and I have a number.

THE MIDDLESEX FELLS.

[*Boston Traveller*, June 23, 1884.]

On the southern border of Middlesex Fells there stands a white oak which measures 10 feet in girth and has a spread of top 62 feet in width. On the northeast corner, in Stoneham, is a group of chestnuts, standing like mother and children, of which the mother is 18 feet and 6 inches in girth. A few white pines may be found standing, probably 80 or 90 feet in height, and over seven feet in girth, and which doubtless grew from the seed within the present century. The remarkable fact is, that many of them stand on solid rock with little, if any, soil under them. This tree, so valuable for lumber, needs only anchorage among the rocks. It grows out of the air. Its nutriment is the gas which makes the air poisonous to breathing animals. Another well-ascertained fact is that the wood of almost any tree increases much faster in its last years than in its first. Doubtless an 80-year-old white pine produces five times as much wood in its eightieth year as in its twentieth. Hence the folly of cutting down clean a white pine forest at 20 years old — or, for that matter, even cutting clean any such forest. Only such trees as have come to maturity should be removed, and their places supplied with seedlings.

THE PUBLIC DOMAIN.

[*Boston Advertiser*, June 20, 1884.]

I am happy to see that the recent outrage on the "Ravine road" has attracted the attention of your correspondent, Mr. J. E. V. Hayden. He is quite right in suggesting that we want something more than picnics,— something more than talk,— something more than the little "Middlesex Fells Association," which never consisted of more than 20 people of small means, and substantially died with John Owen and Wilson Flagg.

The Middlesex Fells Association did not propose to raise money to buy the Fells, but only enough to call public attention to the importance of doing it. It has raised about $300 for this purpose, $212 of which came from the net proceeds of those social entertainments given by ladies; $260 has been expended, and a little over $40 remains at interest in a savings bank. The plan proposed for extinguishing all the individual titles to property in the 4,000 acres desired, which are probably about 200, is to obtain, from persons disposed to aid, "conditional obligations," legally collectible, to pay to a board of trustees, in case the municipalities vote all the land desired, to the satisfaction of a majority of said trustees. On this plan no one is bound to pay anything unless the law is fully carried into effect. A generous subscription in advance of action by the five municipalities, cannot fail to secure favorable action from every one of them. For if anything of a financial nature is certain, it is so, that every one of those municipalities would be the richer by voting for the "public domain" than by not voting for it, if it got no aid from outside. The execution of such conditional obligations has begun, and there are now in the hands of Mr. Henry Brooks, one of the trustees, whose office is at No. 35 Bedford street, Boston, a considerable number of them, ranging in denomination from $2 to $5,000. The smallest of them doubtless bears a higher ratio to the financial ability of the obligor than the largest.

The whole value of the property, land and buildings, which it is proposed to transfer from individuals to the State, probably does not exceed $300,000, and to the present owners, on the average, it does not net 1 per cent.— in fact it hardly yields enough to pay the taxes. As a forest, under scientific management, it may, without any capital but the wood already on the ground, be made to yield a net income larger than if it were all arable. But this is the smallest part of the benefit. It will become at once acceptable to the people of the crowded cities, and be a sanitary resource of a value incalculable in dollars.

Mr. Hayden seems to take it for granted that the Middlesex Fells Association did nothing but *talk* to save the trees on the Ravine road. It may please him to learn that two members of that little body did offer out of their own pockets $1,000 to save them; but in vain. Possibly those health-giving trees were destined to be sacrificed to save their race. If Boston could only see them, as they lie there, tears would flow, if not dollars.

MIDDLESEX FELLS.

[*Boston Advertiser*, July 4, 1884.]

The friends of trees owe thanks to Mr. E. V. Hayden and the Advertiser of July 1 for stating some of the difficulties in the way of converting the Middlesex Fells into a public forest domain. They are doubtless considerable, but not insurmountable. The plan presented may be impracticable, but other plans are possible, and there is always a practicable plan for everything that is really desirable. And a city which has had the wit to effect some far more difficult things, which, comparatively, were not desirable, cannot lack the ingenuity to devise some plan to secure an object which everyone desires, on the score of health as well as pleasure.

Mr. Hayden is perhaps not aware that this subject is not a new one. If he will refer to City Document, No. 123, for 1869, he will see that other plans are possible. One thing in favor of any plan is, that if the entire tract is not put under unitary control, the best water supply of a future population of a million will inevitably be ruined. It must be saved soon, or never.

Mr. Hayden says, truly enough, that "profitable forest culture is incompatible with the purposes of a public pleasure-ground." But he seems to forget that the area in question is large enough to afford the public for pleasure more than New York enjoys in its public park and still have 3,000 acres left sacred to white pine trees under the best scientific management.

Mr. Hayden obviously does not understand what the scientific management of a forest is, for he conceives it to be just what has lately "befallen the woods upon the Ravine road," to wit, an indiscriminate cutting, as with a mowing machine. On the contrary, science only selects for removal such individual trees as have reached their maturity and are retarding the growth of those that would make wood faster, and is careful to plant in their stead trees of the best sort for the place. What it will never do, is to cut down the young trees with the old, or make a dividend wholly or partly out of capital stock. An individual proprietor may do that, forgetful of the fact that, though he owns the trees, he does not own the air which the trees purify. The atmosphere belongs to everybody, and every living being that breathes has an interest in having trees, that effect and preserve its purity, grow on every square rod of surface which cannot be more profitably occupied. The policy of cutting off forests clean, à la Ravine road, was never wise or justifiable on more than three-fourths of the surface of Massachusetts. At least one million of acres was never worth clearing. This is not saying it was or is worthless. But the policy of cutting clean the wood crop once in 20 or 30 years, which has largely prevailed throughout New England, has been too much like that of the man in the fable in regard to his valuable goose.

Every tree gets more sustenance from the air than from the soil. The native white pine hardly needs more from the soil than anchorage against the winds, and birds enough to defend it from insects. What it gets from the air is poisonous to all lungs. It is exactly the tree that will pay us best for a little forethought and care in reinstating it on our sandy plains and rocky hills.

Now, as any schoolboy knows, or ought to know, any healthy tree, from the time of its germination till it reaches its maximum height and expansion, makes wood annually, at a rate somewhere between the square and the cube of its diameter. And after it gets, in the forest, the full height of the forest, it will make wood annually, for a long time, in proportion to its diameter. Hence it is exceedingly wasteful to cut even large trees till, on account of age, they have nearly ceased to grow, and always still more wasteful to cut small ones, unless standing too thick, or being of the wrong kind, till they have reached the full forest height.

It results from these facts that the profit of forest land in Massachusetts, if not throughout New England, is reduced to not more than one-fourth of what it might be, by too early and too indiscriminate cutting, and the neglect of replacing the trees withdrawn by new plants. In other words, we are losing full three-fourths of the possible income from our forest lands for want of that science of forestry which is now in successful application in Europe.

Is there any tariff to protect us against the importation of useful knowledge?

If Mr. Hayden will carefully examine the law by which the Middlesex Fells is to be converted into a public domain, he will see that any wasteful destruction of the trees is thoroughly provided against, and all the net profit that can be made from them is to be returned to the towns that donated the fund.

The plan proposed of encouraging the five municipalities to avail themselves of the law, and put the title in the hands of the State by conditional subscriptions, depends of course on the public spirit of those who approve the object. If Mr. Hayden and others who, like him, think the object desirable, will put before the public a better plan, and urge it as faithfully as Cochituate water was urged against Jamaica Pond, we are sure to have it.

ON THE TOP OF BEAR HILL.

What action; breathing grown to pleasure.
   What rest; to see for once as far
   As eye can see, without a bar,
Except just after those hills without measure
   That belt that level, glassy pond,
   Where *heaven* cuts off the view beyond.

What breezes; sweeping with giant power;
   Then fitfully, coyly skimming the ground—
   Some one is coming you think by the sound,
But it's only the dry leaves. Then up to your tower
   Swells organ music, for straight down below,
   Far underneath you the forest trees grow.

Out of these leagues of green, crowded and packed,
   Some savines have wandered up the hill
   In search of light, with living will,
And found the room for growth they lacked;
   And there they stand now, glorified,
   And of those that dared not *one* has died.

You grow firm with the rocks, and fresh with the trees,
   The tide of life is rising fast
   And ere the bracing wind has past
You are filled with the stronghearted breeze.
   And then you walk quick, to and fro,
   And exult in the deeds you will do below.

What a place to choose as a place to live;
   And what a place as a place to die;
   Looking your last on the earth and sky.
The world doesn't need you to labor or give;
   Only you needed the generous thrill
   Just as poor Stonehamtown needed its hill.

                            LUCY JANE WRIGHT.

FOREST CULTURE FROM A SANITARY POINT OF VIEW.

[*Boston Herald*, Oct. 20, 1884.]

If any reader wants to see what light and color can do for such a planet as this, now is the time. Perch yourself, one of these sunny October days, on some hilltop in the Middlesex Fells. You will never forget it — the gay good-by of the leaves for the winter. The only opponent I have ever found to the "public domain" project, and he is, perhaps, the largest proprietor of territory in the Fells, says to me, "It is a good thing." He only objects to my method of realizing it. I have put the price too low, estimating it at only what the territory is assessed at for taxes. Well, suppose it should cost $1,000,000 instead of $300,000 to extinguish the individual titles to all the property to be transferred to the state, what difference? No property is to be destroyed, only to be made more productive of value, and of all kinds of value, and to a hundred times as many people as now take any comfort out of it. What is a million of dollars to such a state as Massachusetts, to such a city as Boston, even to the five municipalities in which the 4,000 acres of extinct volcano lie, municipalities worth in the aggregate twenty-five or thirty millions of dollars? Once let the thing be done, and the people within 10 miles of it would not have it undone for twenty millions of dollars. It is a boon offered by nature herself to the city of Boston worth more than if it had the fertility of Egypt or of Paradise itself. And this because in most of it no tree will grow to perfection, except white pine. Do you doubt whether the pine forest can be restored to what it was 200 years ago? That is because you have not seen the stumps nor the trees now existing there.

To doubt whether the people of the surrounding towns will ever carry out the act of 1882, chap. 255, in regard to the Middlesex Fells, is to suppose them generally void of rational faculties, and incapable of understanding their own material interests; and to suppose that the most enlightened citizens of Boston will not help them to the extent of a million of dollars if needed, is to assume that the said enlightened citizens are ignorant of the most important fact ever revealed to mankind by the science of chemistry, to wit, that growing trees purify the air. What are all Boston's grand buildings, her crowded workshops, her glowing forges, her interminable lines of horse cars and of iron horses good for if she is to have no sacred forest, where her people who are not very rich can be sure of fresh air — sure of it, for a day at least, for a dime? There may be reasonable doubts on many subjects not yet subjected to experiment, but of the sanitary value of forests in the vicinity of crowded cities there is no more room to doubt than there is that breathing carbonic acid gas is injurious to the lungs. Boston people have already given $5,000,000 to get rid of bad air — will they give nothing to produce good? Will multiplying medicines and medical persons save the multiplying people of Boston's future?

I am often asked, "How are the Fells?" All I have to say is, they are as "willin'" to be yours as Barkis ever was. They are patiently waiting. If you will read chap. 255 of the acts of 1882, you will see how the trees may be saved and multiplied, not only in the Fells, but on all the waste land of the commonwealth, if the people please. That chapter was well considered by a very able committee, and there is no probability of its ever being repealed. If put in practice on the whole 4,000 acres of the Middlesex Fells, the example will be followed on multitudes of other lands throughout the state, where sunshine and rain are now half wasted through ignorance of forest culture. All that needs to be done is to have the people of the immediate vicinity of the Fells come together in social clubs and talk the matter over. This will be done. Already some 200 names of men and women have been secured, mostly in Medford, to act in an organized capacity to promote conditional subscriptions, which will encourage and render certain the requisite vote of the five municipalities to cede the whole territory to the state.

ADDRESS

DELIVERED AT THE ORGANIZATION OF THE MEDFORD PUBLIC DOMAIN CLUB, DECEMBER, 1884.

The difficulty of creating a public domain does not lie in the nature of things; nor in the nature of State government. The thing itself is self-evidently desirable, and so far as State legislation is concerned it already exists. Nature itself has provided a spot and laughs in her sleeve at every attempt to make any other use of it. The remaining difficulty is in accomplishing the needed municipal legislation. The territory lies in five distinct municipalities, and unless all of them concur in ceding to the State the land within their jurisdiction nothing is done. To secure a two-thirds vote in a population of 30,000 or 40,000, divided into five or six separate villages, is by no means an easy matter, and especially in a somewhat novel enterprise, and for an object only to be fully realized in the lapse of a human generation. It has taken a century to destroy the Forests of the Fells, and to reduce them to their present forlorn condition. It will take another to restore them to their pristine luxuriance and grandeur. The first step is to agitate the subject — to talk about it, look at it in all lights, and wake up not only the 40,000 men, women and children nearest to it, but the hundreds of thousands within a dime's ride of it, to see their own interests in the forest which is nothing short of their right and their opportunity to breathe pure air and behold the grandest display of natural scenery. We must multiply public domain clubs, all over the territory within ten miles of the Fells, till we have established what is called a public "craze"— and it will turn out to be the sanest craze that ever took possession of this hub of many crazes.

Very few of the proprietors of the Fells live on their property. Those who do have no control except over what little they own, and even that is more or less injured by risk of fire. What is wanted is a unitary control. In establishing such control, in the name of the State, no private property need be destroyed. The human population will remain about the same, but with different duties. There will be certain permanent residents, fitly distributed, who will get their living by planting and trimming trees, clearing up rubbish, guarding against fires, watching for the purity of the water, seeing that visitors behave themselves with propriety, operating as well qualified forest gardeners, in short.

If the city population, for the benefit of whose lungs the trees grow, cannot breathe among them without committing wanton and malicious injury, it will be because city education has been miserably defective. In fact, just such a forest of ample dimensions, well kept and well policed, is needed to make city education complete. The laws of nature are poorly learned from books. Boston is destined to learn that a great public forest is worth as much as a university. Why should she not have both?

The practicability of restoring the forests so that the highest hill-tops will produce valuable white pines, cannot be doubted by any one who will carefully examine the Fells. All that is wanted is to make two-thirds of the voters believe this.

MIDDLESEX FELLS.

[*Medford Mercury*, Jan. 3, 1885.]

You have done a great service to the Public Domain enterprise by publishing in your last issue the criticism signed L. The arguments in favor of any projected improvement cannot have their proper force, or even be well understood, till all the possible objections are clearly stated. This obvious necessity is well met by L., and calls on the affirmative side for reply.

The critic supposes he floors Mr. Hale on his assertion that "The wealth of the country will be greatly enlarged by the preservation of the forests," by saying, "Certainly not, unless the trees are cut down and used for timber in the coarse and fine arts." He appears to assume that Mr. Hale meant by "preservation" that trees were never to be cut. But this is not quite fair. In the best preserved forests in Europe trees are cut every year, while the forest is not destroyed, just as dividends are, annually or oftener, taken from a bank without impairing the capital. What the Forestry Law endeavors to guard against is treating the timber crop just as we do grass or grain crops, sweeping all down at once. Trees are long-lived. Men, as individuals, are short-lived. Seldom can one who plants a tree wait till it matures. But, as Mr. Hale well said, the State does not die. It can afford to wait till its investment of labor or money can have time to yield its maximum annual return, without destroying the capital. In the meantime the people may enjoy what is worth more than money in the pleasure of looking at the foliage, breathing pure air, and drinking purer water. There are in Massachusetts not less than a million of acres of hill-tops capable of yielding annually more value in timber with less labor, than of either grass or grain. If timber happens to grow on these hill-tops, long before the growth is worthy of the name of forest, it is swept away for cord-wood, and for decades afterwards there is little on the ground but barberry bushes. If the forests were only cared for and preserved on this million of acres of hill-tops — though it might take fifty years to realize it — Mr. Hale might well say that the wealth of the State would be increased, at least, annually, by the amount of the State tax. There is plenty of credible testimony that hills well crowned with forest increase the fertility of the valleys at their feet by a better retention and distribution of the moisture. If Mr. L. doubts this, he has only to read the reports on Forestry of the European governments to learn the general fact.

The critic also calls attention to my feeble and hasty remarks as incongruous, and doubtless with good cause. In saying that the Fells are good for nothing but the pine trees, I meant the *hills*, for that I suppose is the meaning of the word *Fells*. As to the ravines they are generally too narrow if not too rocky to be worth much for farming or gardening. As to the entire tract, I did not mean to say that there are not in it some good farms, fine garden soil, where the black walnut and wild cherry would grow to perfection, all of it naturally and inevitably draining into the water supply. Should these farms be cut up into village lots, and densely populated, what would the water be worth?

My critic well says, "Nature operates on too vast and grand a scale to be influenced by so small a speck as the Middlesex Fells," and he might have said, as Massachusetts. And yet it may be true that a nation of fifty or sixty millions of people, spread over a continent, may by diminishing its forests have considerably affected its climate for the worse, as well as made lumber unnecessarily scarce and dear.

He says, "But observe, the forests have been always the same." This may be true of Massachusetts, for since I have known her many farms have lapsed into bush-pastures, and a few forests have been established. But in regard to the country at large it is by no means true. Sixty years ago, in going from Utica to Cincinnati, how much further I do not know, you saw hardly anything but forest. Now you are in "clearing" about all the way. There is seldom a forest you cannot see through. Many river beds that were always water courses then, are now destitute of water in midsummer. It is very true that the Middlesex Fells is a mere speck in comparison with the continent, but as an example in tree-culture it may be useful to the whole continent. There is no place in the state, except perhaps the top of Blue Hill, where a successful experiment would be more telling. The only question is as to success. Can scientific culture raise valuable timber on the Fells? If it can, then there is no harm in having the scenery beautified and the air and water kept pure.

Mr. L. says he thinks but few would favor such action as would make the Fells a public domain for forests merely as such, "but if a false notion obtained as to the source of water supply, many would be likely to do so, and only see their mistake when too late to remedy it." Now grant — which I do not — that for the sake of tree-culture alone the Public Domain is not needed, let us see about the water supply. Grant that it cannot be increased by increasing the forest. Will Mr. L. pretend that it cannot be kept purer than by letting the population increase, which will necessarily throw its sewage into it? By creating a Public Domain, we are at least sure to keep the water supply as abundant and pure as it is; by *not* doing it, we run the risk of having the quality of the water injured, and to "see our mistake when too late to remedy it."

THE MIDDLESEX FELLS.

[*Boston Herald*, May 11, 1885.]

The grandest and most hopeful sign of these times is the breaking forth of the newspaper press of all political and ecclesiastical parties, in full accord, in favor of tree planting and the preservation of forests. Late last week the New York General Assembly passed almost unanimously a law for the preservation of the Adirondack and other public forests, which the newspapers of all parties approve, and express the hope that the Senate will not defeat.

Massachusetts has not much forest to destroy, but she has a million of acres of hills which ought to be covered with white pines, instead of white birch and discouraged scrub oaks. And she has on her statute book a wise law encouraging her citizens to apply the best scientific culture to the restoration of forests where they are most needed. If the wealth and enterprise of Boston would look into the matter with the foresight and patriotism which some of its citizens showed 100 years ago Boston would ·say to the five towns of Malden, Medford, Stoneham, Winchester and Melrose, "Vote to cede to the commonwealth some $500,000 or less of your taxable real estate for a public domain, and you will not only secure the abundance and purity of your water supply, but I, who through my multitude of citizens shall enjoy the pleasure and salubrity of a 4,000 acre forest of pines and maples, will appropriate all the money necessary to restore the trees as fast as possible."

Now is the time, before the buds of the brush have turned into leaves, to look over the hills of the rugged old crater of perhaps the oldest volcano on the planet, to see whether it is possible to make it as beautiful to look at as the garden of Eden. The brush does not now hide the rocks and the old decaying pine stumps as it will in June. I live in the Fells, and, if called on, shall be happy to show to any practical man the perfect practicability of the project, which will give Boston the finest health and pleasure resort possessed by any city on this globe.

MEN AND TREES.

Animal and vegetable life have a relation to each other as close as that of light and heat. They are utterly different, and yet profoundly alike. The keenest optics have found it difficult to trace the dividing line. The grandest man — poet, philosopher or statesman — feels himself a brother to the grandest tree. His heart expands in view of a well ordered, prosperous, happy society of men, women and children, and hardly less so in view of a primeval forest filling the air with health and joy for all that breathe. For he knows that the republic of trees is the complement of the republic of men, and if the latter does not restrain itself and govern itself wisely in the use of the steel it has so lately discovered, it might as well go back to the stone age.

Human history, developed distinctly only in the last few thousand years, most solemnly and indubitably affirms that, among the chief causes of natural decay, has been the neglect of the forests and the too extensive denudation of the natural covering of the earth's surface. Since Columbus, this devastation of the newly discovered hemisphere has been going on as if history were a false and foolish prophet. Right here in Massachusetts, some of our shrewdest business men say: "No danger about the forests, for we have nearly twice as much woodland as we had 40 years ago." Very true, on the surface, but how is the woodland managed? What sort of trees are planted? What care is taken that they shall be adapted to the nature of the soil? That the fires shall not consume the best, while seedlings, and leave the worst to deceive the eye by their greenness? What care is taken that the valuable young wood shall not be cut off clean like a rye crop, at the very time when it begins to grow rapidly? What care that the best trees shall reach their maturity before they feel the axe?

In harmony with the spirit which is now rising all over the continent in favor of the forests, the latest poem of the aged

Whittier entitled "The Wood Giant," may be considered as a welcome to the forestry congress, which is to assemble for a three days' session in Horticultural Hall on Tuesday of this week. Poetry never rose to a more beneficent use. Its tones ought to re-echo over every hill-top of New England, and clothe the fire-stricken prairies of the West with clusters of forest giants.

THE WOOD GIANT.

BY JOHN GREENLEAF WHITTIER.

From Alton Bay to Sandwich Dome,
   From Mad to Saco river,
For patriarchs of the primal wood
   We sought with vain endeavor.

And then we said : " The giants old
   Are lost beyond retrieval,
This pigmy growth the axe has spared
   Is not the wood primeval.

"Look where we will o'er vale and hill,
   How idle are our searches,
For broad girthed maples, wide limbed oaks
   Centennial pines and birches!

" Their tortured limbs the axe and saw
   Have changed to beams and trestles;
They rest in walls, they float on seas,
   They rot in sunken vessels.

"This shorn and wasted mountain land
   Of underbrush and boulder —
Who thinks to see its full grown tree
   Must live a century older."

At last to us a woodland path,
   To open sunset leading,
Revealed the Anakim of pines
   Our wildest wish exceeding.

Alone, the level sun before,
   Below, the lake's green islands,

Beyond, in misty distance dim,
  The rugged northern highlands.

Dark Titan on his sunset hill
  Of time and change defiant!
How dwarfed the common woodland seemed,
  Before the old time giant.

What marvel that in simpler days
  Of the world's early childhood,
Men crowned with garlands, gifts and praise,
  Such monarchs of the wild wood?

That Tyrian maids with flower and song
  Danced through the hill grove's spaces,
And hoary-bearded Druids found
  In woods their holy places?

With somewhat of that Pagan awe
  With Christian reverence blending,
We saw our pine tree's mighty arms
  Above our heads extending.

We heard his needles' mystic rune,
  Now rising, and now dying,
As erst Dodona's priestess heard
  The oak leaves prophesying.

Was it the half unconscious moan
  Of one apart and mateless,
The weariness of unshared power,
  The loneliness of greatness?

O dawns and sunsets, lend to him
  Your beauty and your wonder,
Blithe sparrow, sing thy summer song
  His solemn shadow under!

Play lightly on his slender keys,
  O wind of summer, waking
For hills like these, the sound of seas
  On far off beaches breaking!

And let the eagle and the crow
  Rest on his still green branches,

When winds shake down his winter snow
In silver avalanches.

The brave are braver for their cheer,
The strongest need assurance,
The sigh of longing makes not less
The lesson of endurance.

Sturtevant's Hill, N. H.

THE DRUIDS ARE COMING.

[*Boston Transcript*, Sept. 16, 1885.]

Among all the religions of the world there is none which had a stronger reason for being than that whose temple was the living forest. It flourished among the ancient Britons and Celts. There is a little remnant of it in Lynn, Mass., where the Laurentian hills have preserved forest enough to prompt the old Druidic worship. The tree is the counterpart of man. The breath of the one is vital to the other. The emotions in man, woman and child, growing out of this fact, have existed time out of mind, ages before history was born. The *why* of the fact was revealed by science hardly more than a century ago. Botany and chemistry have demonstrated beyond a doubt that the leaves of trees as well as their roots are the organs by which they accumulate their solid substance; while all breathing animals, built up by the chemistry of their stomachs, are dependent on the leaves to purify the air from the noxious gases they are constantly throwing off by their lungs.

This discovery and revelation of modern science has revived a practical order of Druids on the North American continent, called the American Forestry Congress. It is none too early. The grandest of American bards, whose bugle blast waked our republic a generation ago from the fatal trance of slavery, now opens the diapason stop of his sublime organ in favor of the tree. Hear him, every father, mother and child in over-crowded Boston —

>   Look where we will o'er vale and hill,
>   How idle are our searches
>   For broad-girthed maples, wide-limbed oaks,
>   Centennial pines and birches!
>
>   Their tortured limbs the axe and saw
>   Have changed to beams and trestles;
>   They rest in walls, they float on seas,
>   They rot in sunken vessels.
>
>   This shorn and wasted mountain land
>   Of underbrush and bowlder —
>   Who thinks to see its full-grown tree
>   Must live a century older.

If you will only listen to what these well taught modern Druids who will assemble at the Horticultural Hall in Boston next Tuesday, the 22d, at ten o'clock, will tell you in three days, we shall not have to wait more than one-third of a century to see both oaks and pines that will be giants in the lifetime of our grandchildren.

THE TREE.

All hail, the buds, the flowers, the leaves,
   All hail, the waking wood,
The summer fruit, the autumn sheaves,
   The pouring out of good.

The sun unlocks the frozen sod,
   And sets the rivers free ;
And lo, half way from man to God,
   Stands worshipping the tree.

The tree, the tree, the blessed tree,
   Without a will but His
Who makes and sets all others free ;
   The tree his high priest is.

It neither hastes nor fears to die,
   But gladdens all abroad
That creep or walk or climb or fly,—
   This almoner of God.

It whispers to the coward soul,
   For shame and you so free,
To fear this death which is the goal
   Of fresher life to be.

THE MASSACHUSETTS FORESTRY LAW.

[*Boston Herald*, Sept. 18, 1885.]

The city of Boston has expended within the memory of middle-aged people many millions of money to supply its citizens with pure water and pure air. Yet "spring water" is sold from carts in the streets, and sewer gas is a nuisance in city palaces; which facts show that there is still much to be learned and done before the best conditions of life are as fully enjoyed as they might be. There has been formed — and none too early — an association of scientific men which calls itself the American Forestry Congress, whose object is to promote the preservation and reproduction of forests over the whole continent. They recognize the alarming fact that in a large part of the United States and Canada the people are increasing faster than the trees; that in multitudes of our growing cities it is becoming more and more difficult to supply the people with either pure water or pure air — which are the greatest interests that mankind hold in common.

The people, from the highest to the lowest, must begin to think on this subject.

Some wise thinking was done by our Legislature in 1882, when it placed on the statute book chap. 255. It authorizes town meetings and city boards, by a two-thirds vote, to set apart territory for the preservation and reproduction of forests, the individual titles to be extinguished in the same manner as if the land were taken for roads. And provision is made in the laws for the best scientific treatment of the public domains so created. The forestry congress meets in the Horticultural Hall in this city, at the invitation of the world-famous society which owns that favorite building, and of all the state societies for the promotion of agriculture, including that which, under the act above referred to, is constituted the board of forestry.

THE MIDDLESEX FELLS.
[*Boston Herald*, Oct. 12, 1885.]

Sixty-one years ago last May, it was my lot to journey by stage coach from Andover to Boston on the old Andover turnpike. It was a glorious ride, for the day was splendid, and I was green, and so were the surroundings. Just out of my teens, in the wild west, I wondered to see what little bits of fields the people were ploughing for corn by the roadside, among bowlders thicker than the big stumps in Ohio. I saw much woodland, bordering the field, but small wood. As I approached Boston, I expected to see more cultivation. But from Stoneham to Medford there was less. For several miles almost none. There were glimpses of a beautiful sheet of water. There were here and there clumps of white pines and hemlocks. But mostly rude havoc of the axe, replaced by birch and oak brush. There were everywhere stone walls, showing that agricultural industry had, some time or other, laid out farms and failed. Nature had done its best to conceal the failure. Here was evidently a large piece of land, almost within a stone's throw of Boston, which in regard to human habitations, had been thrown down by nature like a big skim-milk cheese into a pig-sty, which an apt English rhymer said was "too big to swallow and too hard to bite." There was a mystery about it. It will have to be solved some time or other.

Grand old William Foster of Summer street bought 200 acres of the tract, and built a sweet little French chateau on the eastern border of Spot pond, and tried to entice his neighbors to do the same. He succeeded with two or three. But it was prior to the iron horse. He became discouraged, and gave away his land to the Franklin Institute, which allowed it to be sold for taxes. It was soon denuded by the wood-chopper.

About fifteen or sixteen years ago, when there was some agitation in Boston for more room for the people to breathe, play and enjoy themselves in, it was seriously proposed that the city should buy this whole tract of about 4,000 acres, fertilize a part by clothing it with the Mystic mud, and convert the rest into a grand park for the recreation of the future people. Too much could be done for too little money. (See City Document No. 123, 1869.)

For several years past, under the lead of the venerable John Owen, Mr. Longfellow's fidus Achates, and the enthusiastic naturalist, Wilson Flagg, the public has been considerably stirred up to see the grandeur of the opportunity for future generations of this wonderfully persistent remnant of a pine forest. These leaders are, sad to relate, both dead. Their labors resulted, in 1882, in a law which allows the people of any town or city, by a two-thirds vote, to cede to the state any land on which they wish the forest to be restored or preserved. Should such a vote take place concurrently in the five municipalities which embrace the Middlesex Fells the proprietors will have to look to the courts for the value of their real estate, as if the land had been taken for roads. Under the provision which the law makes for the care of the land and the water those municipalities will be far richer than they were before. There is, in fact, no other way in which that land can become other than a nuisance but by such a concurrent vote at the earliest possible time.

A movement is already on foot, of individual speculation, which, unless the law of 1882 can be carried out next spring by a concurrent vote of the one city and four towns, will result in destroying all hope of a forest or pure water from either Spot pond or the Winchester reservoirs. Shall half a dozen men defeat some thirty thousand people and their posterity from the best chance of pure air and clear water, that they may make a trifle more profit? Boston and the entire state are interested in this question, for, if the Middlesex Fells public domain fails, millions of other acres in Massachusetts which might bear profitable forests will be left to mere shabbiness. No son of the old Bay state will ever want to come back to the bald hills where the masts of the old navies grew, to end his days under the bitter Northeasters.

AN INTERESTING COMMUNICATION ON FORESTRY.

[*Medford Mercury*, Oct. 30, 1885.]

Your correspondent "L.," of West Medford, has certainly laid your readers under great obligations by his extended discussion of "Forestry and Pure Water." I am glad to hear a man of such general information say, that "the project of the purchase of the Fells seems to be in a precarious state of incubation." Incubation is good. It is a natural and necessary process for the production of the sublimest of animated beings. But for incubation, more or less precarious, where would have been that successful bird, which we are wont to take pride in, as our bird of Freedom?

Your correspondent seems to think that the farmers of Massachusetts, who own the woodlands, will take the best possible care of them for their own interests, and so the wisest thing is to let them severely alone. And yet we have agricultural societies, and an agricultural committee in every legislature, just as if farmers needed to know more about the cultivation of common annual crops. Only three years ago, the agricultural committee had before it for nearly the whole session a bill which became Chapter 255 of the Acts of 1882. It had special reference to the tract of land between Malden and Winchester, chiefly in Stoneham and Medford, called the "Middlesex Fells." But the act is general for the state, and authorizes any town or city to cede to the state tract within its territory, "for the preservation, reproduction and culture of forest trees, for the sake of the wood or timber thereon, or for the preservation of the water supply of such town or city — subject to the regulations hereinafter prescribed." No bill ever passed by the General Court was more deliberately or thoroughly discussed by the men representing the farmers of Massachusetts. The utmost care was taken that the private rights of individual proprietors should be perfectly protected. Possibly a city government, *if it had within its own territory* a suitable place, might be so monomaniacal as to surround its water supply with forests, regardless of expense, but two-thirds of the voters in any town must be monomaniacs to do it. The legislature evidently did not deem it possible there should be so many in one town, especially if there should be in that town a citizen so expert in water supply as your correspondent " L." The law is therefore not only safe and prudent, but it would be so, if the monomaniacs were much increased.

No voter of either of the five municipalities interested in the Middlesex Fells, however confident that the devotion of the whole tract to a public domain, for the purposes of the law, would be a public benefit, to both the near and the remote future, would give it his vote, on any other condition than that all the municipalities should concur. For any one to refuse to accept the law, would ruin the whole affair. This is self-evident. On the other hand, if all accept it, the aggregate property of all, and of every one, would be largely increased. In the first place, the one or two hundred proprietors in the land included in the tract devoted, will, if they do not donate it, be paid its just cash value. Second, the thousands of citizens who own property in the five municipalities outside of the Fells, will have it more or less raised in value, made in fact more salable, probably in a few years doubled in value. You own a dwelling and lot in one of those beautiful villages on the borders of the beautiful pine forest of the future. Its price will rise as the beauty and success of the grand experiment draws visitors from Boston and the world. Now don't let any financial dolt make you believe that the increase of taxes is going to cancel the increase of value. You would not refuse an addition as a gift to your land or your house, if you needed it, for fear it would be taxed. Taxes do not commonly take the principal, but only a part of the interest on the value. If people vote wisely they will increase the value of their property out of proportion to the increase of the taxes.

Again I take the liberty to call the attention of every

thinking man and woman in the neighborhood of the singularly abused Middlesex Fells, to the theories, criticisms, arguments and recommendations about water supply, of your correspondent "L." Give them the fullest and frankest consideration, because they interest all who are to come after you. You will observe that he talks about pure water rather despondently, unless you dig 300 or 400 feet for it. But he omits the subject of *pure air* which we are more dependent upon than we are on pure water. As if a man of such vast acquirements of knowledge could be ignorant of the fact, discovered a little more than a century ago, that it is the forest which absorbs the carbon out of the carbonic acid produced by lungs and furnaces, and liberates the oxygen, and thus sustains the life of cities and nations.

FAS EST AB HOSTE DOCERI.

[*Medford Mercury*, Nov. 1, 1885.]

If ways of wisdom you have kenned,
Your enemy may be your friend.

When the white-skin landed on this coast, the trees were his enemies. They occupied nearly the whole surface. He had to exterminate them right and left. His axes and saws left only here and there one for its shade; and that, tall and alone, soon blew down. Only the hill-tops saved anything like a forest; and time and fire made great havoc of that. There was no aristocracy of sportive hunters to preserve the forests for the sake of the game. So the trees, especially on the levelest and richest part of the republic, have dwindled away as men have multiplied. In this hilly New England there is so little really arable land, and the people have had such large families, that if some had not gone west, and others, who stayed at home, had not learned to make more shoes and clothes than they wanted to wear themselves, a good many must have starved to death. Thanks to canals and railroads, a man who can make a pair of good boots in Massachusetts can buy from Minnesota more flour for the same, than he could raise on any acre in Massachusetts, even if he owned the acre. So there is no excuse for a Minnesota man if he goes without boots, nor for the Massachusetts man if he does not favor the utmost cultivation and preservation of trees.

It is very probably truly said, that Massachusetts has twice as many acres of wood land as it had forty years ago; and it might be said with even greater probable truth, that it has not one-quarter as much wood. The reasons of this are: first, that the cultivation of cereal crops is not so remunerative as it was; second, that trees are cut for fuel or lumber before they have attained their full growth; third, that little if any labor is bestowed in planting the proper kind of trees on land that is liberated from agriculture; fourth, that almost no pains is taken to prevent the fires that burn leaves yearly and destroy the seedlings of all those trees which do not sprout from the roots; fifth, the doctrine so carefully instilled into nearly all farmers, that when a pine forest is cut away it must necessarily be succeeded by a forest of deciduous trees. This is a pernicious falsehood, for there is not a hill-top in the commonwealth which will not bear the white pine as well or better than any other kind of tree, as long as it stands, pine after pine, if only the seeds are planted and protected from fire till they grow beyond its reach. Every sort of tree should be put in the conditions of soil and air most favorable to it. A very little of well established science applied to the million acres of hills in Massachusetts would within forty years make them yield more value in wood per acre, and with far less labor, than any acres of wheat land in Minnesota.

TO THE PEOPLE OF MEDFORD, MALDEN, MELROSE, STONEHAM AND WINCHESTER.

The MIDDLESEX FELLS is a territory of nearly four thousand acres, quite unequally divided among the five municipalities above named. The people of those five municipalities are all interested in the region, very nearly in proportion to their present and future numbers, whether they, or any of them, are individual proprietors or not.

One thing is perfectly certain. If the whole of this region were devoted to a public domain, under the contract provided by the laws of 1882, for making the most of the water supply by promoting the largest possible growth of the trees, the real estate left to the five municipalities would be of greater value than the whole is now, and in a few years, of many times greater value. It is a use of these comparatively waste lands which cannot be neglected by the people of these five municipalities, as a whole, without incalculable loss to themselves and their posterity. It is·throwing away the best chance of pure air, and almost the only chance of pure water for drinking and cooking within their reach. If the opportunity presented by the law of 1882 is not seized soon, by all the five municipalities in concert,—for doing it by a part would only hasten the evil,—population will pour in, and the defilement of the common water supply will be inevitable and irreparable. If the whole of the water which falls on the Middlesex Fells, by the average rainfall, can be saved, it will be sufficient not only to nourish the densest forest of pines but to furnish, as may be easily calculated, to a million of people, for every day of the year, four imperial gallons of pure water apiece. Sea water is good enough to sprinkle the streets and etxinguish fires, and river water is good enough to wash clothes, but pure water, the purest that earth can afford, is a necessity of life. Shall the multitudes that are to live in sight of these rocky hills, in coming years, die of thirst? Shall they curse their fathers for throwing away an opportunity which will now cost them comparatively nothing — one year's taxes at most? If the people of these five municipalities are to be saved, they must look into this matter and save themselves. It is nonsense to expect other governments, or rich persons elsewhere to save them. They must muster every voter in town meeting and vote themselves safe! Pure water and pure air, for drinking and breathing purposes, are necessaries of health, if not of life. When a population becomes dense they are only secured with forethought and care and concert of action. Forests, if properly cared for, will secure both of these prime necessities for any amount of population which may hereafter inhabit the valleys of Massachusetts. But if the hills are not clothed with the best trees that will grow on them, the springs will in a great measure dry up, the rivers will not only decrease, but become impure and sources of disease, and both population and civilization will wane.

A law was placed on our statute book in 1882, of the most vital importance to five municipalities in the neighborhood of Boston, by which if their people will agree to act in concert, the large water shed of what has been called the Middlesex Fells, may be secured forever, not only as a vast reservoir of Forest purified air, but of water of the greatest possible purity, sufficient to supply a million of mouths, daily, with four imperial gallons apiece. The purpose of the law can only be accomplished by all these municipalities acting in concert, at the earliest moment. It will be defeated by delay, or any partial action.

The law which authorizes any municipality of this Commonwealth by a two-thirds vote to devote land to the purpose of preserving the forests and protecting the supply of pure water, is probably the most important on the statute book, and the immediate application of it to the Middlesex Fells, a large tract in the city of Malden and the towns of Stoneham, Medford, Melrose and Winchester, is the most important case under it, because unless that tract can be very soon converted into a public domain, it will be forever too late. Already a movement is on foot to erect buildings and make avenues which will introduce a population inconsistent with the preservation of the forests or the purity of the water. It is essential that before any such investments are made, the interests of the people surrounding the Middlesex Fells, in the water and the woods, as provided for by the Law of 1882, shall be secured.

TO LAKE WINNIFRED, *NEE* GULL LAKE.

Thou forest gem, green of a thousand lakes,
Around whose pebbled shores the song awakes
Of myriad birds that hail the gladdening dawn;
Whose water mirrors all the sky, and slakes
The noontide thirst of timid doe and fawn;
Whose pine-crowned hills o'erlook the forest sweep,
See gay processions o'er and in the deep,
And on the hither shore the emerald meads
And long drawn points, whose flowers and trees caress
The crystal waters in their gala dress.
But not a house in all the vista round,
Except a single prehistoric mound
Where man has haply slept ten thousand years,
And only one small bark appears,
O mighty fountain, what shall be thy fate
A score of decades from this date?
Shall she who loved the birds and flowers and trees
Become the Empress of these mimic seas?
Shall she who sang the songs of all the larks
And danced, as dance across the waves the barks,
Invite from every clime the young to come
And share the worship of her spirit home?

TO THE DEPARTMENT OF THE INTERIOR.

[*Boston Worker*, July 29, 1879.]

In traversing the great lumber regions of the Northwest, as I have repeatedly in the last three years, I have been struck with the necessity of some speedy action on the part of the General Government to prevent the destruction by forest fires of the young growing timber which belongs to the public domain. The preservation of the forests is a public care in the old countries, and ought to be in ours. The axe of the lumberman is making great havoc and waste, but that is nothing to the fires which are made utterly destructive of the young trees by his leaving the tops of those he fells for the saw, to become dry combustibles.

Forest fires, in the pine lands do comparatively little mischief except where the lumberman has left a multitude of tree tops. This is generally in the vicinity of harbors and water-courses by which the logs are floated or "driven" to market. To save the timber left standing every tree top should at once be converted into cord-wood or put into a shape in which it can be protected from fire till it can be carried where it is needed as fuel. If it is said this operation for the sake of the fuel itself would not pay — it cannot be said that it would not pay when we take into account the saving of the standing timber.

The Government that owns the vast and valuable property endangered, can well afford to make it profitable to save this fuel. Here is a large opening for Labor, which requires no great amount of skill; and as these pine forests are interspersed with lakes of the purest water, abounding in fish, and meadows yielding excellent grass for cattle, good sites for social colonies may be had without having to clear anything but here and there a patch of the deciduous woods which occupy very fertile spots. The light soils in which the pines grow should never be cleared, as the tree crop, if the growth is properly encouraged, will be more profitable than wheat.

I think if a proper representation were made to the next Congress on the subject, it would result in a policy of special encouragement to the colonization of those timber lands under proper regulations for the sake of the timber. It would be easy in the present redundancy of the laboring population in the cities to establish, in a season or two, colonies throughout the great pine forests of the North-west which would entirely put an end to the destructive forest fires.

The colonies would be much insulated to be sure from each other, but would easily have mail facilities connecting them with the great world ; and each of them would soon be a summer resort of worthy people from the cities in search of pleasure — boating, fishing or gunning.

The large landholders and the great land-grant railroads as well as the government are interested in having a colonization of this kind effectual.

THE MISSISSIPPI DAMS.

THE OBJECT OF A PROJECTED CRIME.— SOMETHING ABOUT THE LANDS IN MINNESOTA, AND WHAT THEY ARE GOING TO BE GOOD FOR.

[*Boston Herald*, Aug. 4, 1882.]

The president in his excellent veto of the river and harbor bill says he approves of the appropriations for the improvement of the Potomac flats and the Mississippi river. But I do not think he meant to include, in his approval of the latter, the following: "For reservoirs at the headwaters of the Mississippi river, continuing operations, $300,000."

His principal objection to the bill was: "That it contains appropriations for purposes not for the common defence or general welfare, and which do not promote commerce among the states. These provisions, on the contrary, are entirely for the benefit of the particular localities in which it is proposed to make the improvements." This making reservoirs by damming the headwaters of the Mississippi, is most emphatically exposed to the President's objection.

First — Because it has never been satisfactorily shown that the reservoirs can improve the navigation of the Mississippi. The surveying engineers who have favored the scheme do not pretend it will have any effect below Lake Pepin.

Second — It will not even benefit the localities in which it is proposed to make the dams. On the contrary, it will vastly injure those localities by drowning valuable meadows and timber, and probably creating nuisances which will render thousands of square miles of the best land uninhabitable.

As to the seven dams proposed north of the Northern Pacific railroad, on which the army engineers have been at work surveying and estimating since 1870, at an expense of considerably more than $50,000, they have estimated the cost of construction at $336,458.60, without including a cent for land damages, and any one at all acquainted with the country, either from actual observation or from reading the admirable geological survey made under the direction of David Dale Owen in 1847-8 and 9, must know that the damages to the land — whoever now owns it — must, by more than 10 times, exceed the estimated cost of construction. I will give from the engineer's report the cost of constructing those various dams — without using the silent letter naturally suggesting itself.

1. Lake Winnibigoshish	.	$59,769.80
2. Leech lake	.	55,000.00
3. Mud lake	.	31,737.20
4. Mouth of Vermillion	.	56,245.20
5. Pokegama falls	.	75,334.00
6. Pine river	.	32,386.20
7. Gull lake	.	25,786.20
Total cost	.	$336,458.60

THE CENTS IN SUCH AN ESTIMATE give to the bulk of readers an appearance of precision, but involve a flavor of professional humbug. But possibly the whole cost may be 60 cents less than the estimate. Whether so or not, it will be a bagatelle to the damage. To give some idea of the latter, I will ask the reader's attention to two or three paragraphs, extracted from the Report of the Chief of United States Engineers for 1879, part II., p. 1199 ·

> Gull Lake dam. To cost $25,786.20. Of this the same officer (J. D. Skinner) reports : The system of lakes of which Gull lake is the centre and which discharge their water into Crow Wing river through Gull Lake river, form an excellent storage for water. The discharge of Gull Lake river was, on the 10th of November last, 330 feet per second. The area of the watershed of Gull river, above the outlet of Gull lake, is 7,582,924,800 square feet (meaning as much as 174,000 acres); and, assuming that one-third of the annual rainfall can be collected in the reservoirs and discharged therefrom, we would have 5,262,920,000 cubic feet. The area of Gull and adjacent lakes, that can be used for storage purpose, is 501,841,200 square feet (about 11,521 acres), on which the water can be stored for an average depth of 10 feet, and 223,027,200 square feet, on which an average depth of 5 feet can be stored, giving a total capacity of 6,133,548,000 cubic feet. A dam 12 feet high can easily be constructed to obtain the above capacity of reservoir.

It is plain enough to any one that the engineers charged with this business could not have measured the watershed so as to be sure of its area within several thousand acres, nor the area of the lakes to be sure of it within some hundreds of acres. But, supposing their estimates correct enough for practical purposes, it is quite plain that their 12-foot dam will retain their assumed rainfall.· But what of the damage to the land to be overflowed? By their own admission of an average five-foot depth, there must be at least 5,120 acres, outside of the lake margins, to be overflowed. And while the upland, which will not be overflowed, is generally very light and sandy, fit only for the growth of pines, the low lands that must be overflowed is of the richest soil to be found in the state, covered with the most nutritious grasses and heavy sugar maple, birch, basswood and oak. This land is probably all of it within 20 miles of a railroad, and some of it within five. It only needs CULTIVATORS AND A MARKET to be worth $100 an acre. Here, then, is a land value of over $500,000 which belongs to the future, to be destroyed entirely, to say nothing of the malarial fevers to be suffered by those who may populate the surrounding country. This is the least costly and probably the smallest of the seven projected reservoirs, so that we may fairly suppose that the land damage of the seven will amount to seven times as much, or at least $3,500,000.

But this would be only the smallest part of the mischief. The engineers reporting in favor of it themselves say: "The probability is that the creation of reservoirs will prove of benefit, generally, to the logging interest." Of course it will. Senator Beck of Kentucky told the Senate in the discussion which took place July 7 that, on account of his interest in a similar scheme to improve the navigation of the Ohio, he had been twice to the upper Mississippi to look into this matter of dams, and once as far up as he could go without wading, and he was fully satisfied that it could be of no possible use except to help the floating of logs to Minneapolis. Do the lumber speculators, who leave the tree tops to be wasted where they fall, to dry up and kindle fires which destroy all the trees of the future, deserve to be helped at such a cost? The watershed of the Mississippi, north of the Northern Pacific in Minnesota, contains over 5,000 square miles, or 3,200,000 acres, and most of it is the finest timber land this side of the Rocky mountains, interspersed with rich meadows and lakes of the purest water, abounding in fish, water fowl and wild rice. The railroad managers have sold on the stump vast quantities of lumber growing on land granted to them by the government to speculators, who do not seem to have been very careful about lines dividing railroad from government sections. They only need to be helped, as these seven dams will help them, to destroy in 10 years all the trees growing on soil which, when cleared, they say is "so light that a warrantee deed won't hold it." The policy of the railroad men has been to send all emigrants as far West as possible on to the prairies, where their teeth must chatter in the winter for want of the fuel wasted on the first 150 miles of the road. They tell them timber land is worthless. But LET US SEE ABOUT THAT.

In a single year the Northern Pacific received $100,000 for lumber sold on the stump. At the present prices of lumber it is easy to prove that the annual growth of wood in such forests is of greater net value than that of wheat on the best prairie land. It only requires science and care not to waste the capital of growth. The fertile land to be found among the upper Mississippi forests will easily support a population to keep the forests in the state of highest production.

The same truth may be inferred from the very report of the United States engineer already quoted from. One of the duties imposed upon the engineer corps was to estimate the land damages incident to the scheme. Not a figure can I find devoted to that branch of the subject, and the excuse for this neglect is extremely significant. In relation to the seven dams above specified, the following is all I find in the report:

"The land overflowed is almost entirely on the Indian reservation above the Vermillion dam. There is no land under cultivation, but some hay meadow would be submerged, and the wild rice, on which the Chippewas largely subsist, would, for a few seasons, be drowned out. This, however, would probably find its way to the surface in time, and be as luxuriant as ever. Below Vermillion river are extensive meadows along the river, owned by lumbermen, from which they derive annually their hay for their stock during their winter logging operations. This, after the erection of the dam at Pokegama falls, would be cut off and the meadows ruined. Hay, however, could be obtained elsewhere, though with less convenience. Of course, provision would have to be made for the passage of logs through the several dams. This is all the damage that could be sustained, the country being entirely given up to Indians and lumbermen." Thus we see that the lumbermen will be more than compensated for the loss of their meadows by the greater convenience of floating their logs, and the Indians have no rights which a white government is bound to respect. But what about the white people of the future, of whose land the government is the guardian? Are their interests to be sacrificed in advance for the convenience of timber thieves?

But THE STATE OF MINNESOTA HAS SOME RIGHTS and a good deal of school land to be overflowed. The House, in passing the bill, put in the following proviso, which was struck out in the Senate: "And provided, further, that the states of Minnesota and Wisconsin shall cede to the United States exclusive jurisdiction over the land so taken during the time the same may be used for the purposes herein stated." I am personally acquainted with that most peculiar and interesting region to a considerable extent, and have much more to say. But I will close with a quotation from David Dale Owen's report about the wild rice, which I have had the pleasure to taste and to see where it grows. It was cooked by a woman from the state of Maine. In regard to THE PRODUCTIONS OF THE SOIL on the extreme head waters of the Mississippi, Mr. Owen says (see his report, p. 324):

"Above this, the channel of the river winds through rice fields, amounting in all to several hundred acres. Of all this, the produce of scarcely an acre is gathered by the Indians. When it is considered that an acre of this rice is nearly or quite equal to an acre of wheat for sustaining life, the waste of breadstuff in this region, from the indolence and improvidence of the Indians, can be understood. In this connection it may not be out of place to remark that, so far as the mere support of life is concerned, taking into account the amount of labor required to do it, this region is equal, if not superior, to many portions of the settled states. The rice fields, which require neither sowing nor cultivation, only harvesting, cover many thousands of acres, and yield all that is essential for breadstuff; but, in addition to this, corn can be cultivated with as little or less labor than in the middle states. Potatoes, far superior in size and flavor to any I have ever seen in the Ohio valley, are grown with little attention, and turnips and beets produce abundantly. Extensive natural meadows border the lakes and streams, the luxuriant grasses of which are sweet and nutritious, and eagerly eaten by cattle, while the streams and almost innumerable lakes abound with a great variety of fish of the finest quality, and which may be taken at all seasons with little trouble. The uplands are generally covered with a good growth of both hard and soft woods, sufficient for all the wants of man. The sugar maple is abundant; sufficiently so to yield a supply of sugar for a large population. In addition to all this, the forests are stocked with game, and the lakes and rice fields must always, as they do now, attract immense flocks of water fowl."

Could the President and Congress do better than to save all this from being sacrificed to the greed of speculators in lumber?

THE UNITED STATES AT WAR WITH THE FORESTS,

IN THE INTEREST OF MANUFACTURERS OF LUMBER.
DAMAGES OF DAMS.

[*Boston Sun.*]

Nine or ten years ago Congress set the War Department at surveying the waters of the Mississippi above the mouth of the Crow Wing, with the professed object of creating a number of reservoirs to hold back the water in the wet season for the benefit of the navigation when the water should otherwise become too low. In 1875 the army engineers reported that they had projected and surveyed seven dams, and estimated the cost of construction, as follows:

1.	At the outlet of Lake Winnibigoskish	$50,769.80
2.	Leech Lake	55,000.00
3.	Mud Lake	31,797.20
4.	Mouth of Vermillion	56,245.20
5.	Pokegama Falls	75,334.00
6.	Pine River	32,286.00
7.	Gull Lake	25,786.20

No appropriation was made for the construction of any of these dams till 1880, when about one quarter of a million of dollars was added to estimate of cost, and $75,000 was appropriated for the construction of the Winnibigoskish dam as an experiment.

Without waiting to see how the experiment turned out, whether there was any damage done to wood lands or health by the overflow, or whether the dam would hold water or not, Congress appropriated $150,000 more in 1881 for the dams generally, to be applied where the Secretary of War should see fit, and in 1882 it appropriated $300,000 more. Thus it has appropriated $525,000 without any experimental evidence that the dams will do anything whatever, except to facilitate the floating of saw logs from a larger area of forest to the mills in Minneapolis and higher up the river.

Now all that the very able army engineers have promised is, that if the seven dams are completed and the reservoirs created are kept full till the dry season in the latter part of summer, their contents will make the Mississippi navigable below St. Paul as far down as Lake Pepin. But among the specifications for all these dams are sluice ways for the passage of saw logs. These cannot be used without liberating a good deal of water, which will refuse to run back into the reservoir for the benefit of the future navigation below St. Paul. The lumbermen having the benefit of the impounded water of the lakes and streams, will be sure to use it as soon as the ice melts in the spring, and the practical problem of how much will be left to help navigation in the month of August remains to be solved. One thing is quite certain, that while logs are floated loose, and not in booms, between the falls of Pokegama and St. Anthony, steamboat navigation between those points will not be helped by the dams. There is nothing a steamboat is more afraid of than breaking its motive organs on a floating log. It is not the log that suffers. Hence, whatever navigation there is above Minneapolis must be destroyed by the dams.

Whether it was constitutional or not, Congress has been very kind and generous to the millers of Minneapolis in helping them since 1870 to the amount of over $600,000 — $200,000 of which was wasted in useless work — to prevent their magnificent water power from going up stream out of their reach. Is that a good reason why Congress should spend as much more to aid the lumber manufacturers? They do not need, or to any great extent use, water power to convert logs into boards. Steam, raised by the débris of the logs themselves, does it. Not a log needs to be floated further down the Mississippi than to the Northern Pacific Railroad before it is sawed. And if Congress is not foolishly, not to say unconstitutionally generous, the lumbermen themselves will build all the dams they need without the danger of destroying by overflow living trees, hay, and wild rice, and creating a malaria that will destroy themselves. What Congress has to do, if it does anything, is to prevent the lumbermen from destroying the forests, by obliging them to carry off or burn upon the spot, at a safe time, all the débris of the trees they cut, otherwise the said débris, in a dry time, becomes kindling, which has only to catch to destroy ten or a hundred times as many live pines as the lumbermen have themselves. We have already had in the great pine forests of this country too many Peshtigo fires to make our neglect and abuse of our forests anything less than a national crime.

The limit which Congress set in the appropriation bills to the sums to be paid out of the appropriations for damages by overflow not being more than 10 per cent. of the same, should have prevented the expenditure of a single dollar in construction. If the Leech Lake Indian reservation were the property of white proprietors, the right of flowage of the two reservoirs on that tract could not be purchased of them for less than twice the cost of the dams. Besides destroying the hay meadows and the wild rice, a most excellent and nutritious food which grows spontaneously on hundreds of acres, the reservoirs must drown and kill hundreds of acres of hard wood growing on the fertile low lands, causing by the malaria the whole territory to be worthless, except for human graves. It was with the utmost good sense that the 3,000 Indians dwelling on that reservation, rejecting with scorn the paltry pittance of less than $18,000 which was offered them for damages, are now demanding, with knives under their blankets, not less than $500,000 a year for the destruction of about all they have to eat, and the chance of being victims of fever and ague the rest of their lives.

Is it not plain that this sort of dam, whether the pretences be true or false, won't do?

REPORT

ON THE PROBABLE EFFECT UPON THE FORESTS OF THE SEVEN DAMS ON THE UPPER MISSISSIPPI.

Your Committee, charged to report on this subject, can report no actual effect, because neither of the seven reservoirs projected on the head waters of the great river has been so far filled as to immerse trees standing on the banks. We have, however, made such examination, to be detailed by and by, of the country embraced within the grasp of the Mississippi and the Crow Wing, as to be sure that if all the reservoirs are filled and kept full each year till July, up to the designed elevation above ordinary low water of from eight to fourteen feet, an absolutely large amount of forest as well as valuable rice lakes and grass land must be submerged, at the risk, more or less, of making the country less desirable for settlement. Compared with the whole area, that which will be submerged in consequence of the dams will certainly be small, because the lake area to be covered by the reservoirs is very large. Most of the territory is covered by plains and hills of sand or sandy gravel, excellently adapted to the growth of pine timber; and by far the most of the oak cedar, tamarac, maple, basswood, ash, elm, poplar, birch, &c., on the low land is where none of these reservoirs can molest these trees.

Three dams have been constructed and substantially completed at an expense of considerably over half a million dollars, and tested to the extent of holding back the water to a height of about two and a half feet, and are probably strong enough to hold it to the designed height for five or six years, when the wooden part, which rests upon piles driven below air, will have to be replaced with stone and iron at perhaps greater expense. As these dams are experimental it was wise to make the experiment with wood; and it has been made with the best wood a magnificent forest could furnish, put together with the best engineering skill.

It is far from your Committee to say that if the results to the navigation of the lower river are to be realized, the cost has been too great. The figures of the chief engineer, however, do not seem to demonstrate that the results hoped for will be realized to the extent expected, even if the reservoirs are filled any more than that they will be filled. Too many variables of unknown magnitude are left out of the calculation, such as soil absorption and early summer evaporation. It is assumed that because so many billions of cubic feet of water is found to flow by the dam-site previous to July in a state of nature, just so much may be impounded by the dam, and be ready to help navigation after that date. All that does not necessarily follow, because sand banks are bibulous when the frost is out : raise the water to their lips and they will drink, especially in June. Naturally the waters stand or run in basins or channels substantially of clay, and consequently in a state of nature the earth absorption is at a minimum. As the water rises in the reservoirs, the absorption by the sand banks reached must increase, and that this absorption proceeds laterally is proved by many sandy lakes in this region which have no visible outlets.

But it is the object of our report to criticise the reservoir system only in the interest of the forests, on the flourishing existence of which, this Congress will certainly agree, the river itself mainly depends. Let us admit that the dams are a hydrostatic success, and accomplish everything hoped for. It is undeniable that there must be for some years such a submergence and alternate exposure to the air of trees, as has in all other climates, caused wide-spread and intolerable malaria. This will be proportionally less for the three dams already completed than for the four that are to be. And it may be said that there is little population in their neighborhood to be afflicted. There will be the dam tenders and the Indians, anyhow. Will it not be well for Congress to wait and see what the effect is on them before building any more dams?

One thing is certain, that the reservoirs will not obstruct the ravages of the lumber men or of the fires. The former do not spare anything within their reach which can be converted into boards, shingles, telegraph poles or railroad ties. The débris dries and burns the rest. The traveller is saddened by passing through stately groves of the most valuable pines, dead and delivered to the beetles. The fires did it. Even the living trees which the lumber men are glad to take, have been much injured by brush fires. There cannot be on 5,000 square miles more than half the lumber value there would have been but for the fires.

If the government owning most of this land, could afford, for the sake of the future navigation of the river, to spend a million or two of dollars, surely it can afford for the preservation of the forests as well as the river, to spend as much more to put into every township of 36 square miles, such a colony of families as would effectively prevent forest fires, and replant valuable trees as fast as any are taken away. A

well-organized population of 50,000 foresters would not only
support themselves, but prevent fires, and restore the forest
to its highest productiveness. It would only be necessary
to open convenient roads, build suitable lookouts and telephones, give each colony of five or ten families the use of a
square mile of land — and this land could often be found
very easy to clear. Many of the lakes yield fine fish; the
smaller ones abound in wild rice, which could be made more
abundant; and fine pasturage for cattle, with hay meadows
for their wintering, abound everywhere. The jack pine, good
for nothing but fencing and fuel, is too abundant almost
everywhere. It seems as if even our American Congress
might be made to see that the preservation and restoration
of the great Mississippi Forest is as easy — as "falling off a
log"— and inasmuch as it is the very breath of the future,
the dearest interest of every man, woman and child in this
democratic republic, it must be as much within the power of
Congress to do it, as to spend money for the benefit of
steamboat owners from St. Paul to Lake Pepin, or lower.

But the benefits, sorely needed benefits, of the reservoir
system are capable of being set forth, and have been set
forth so brilliantly as to charm the public mind. Every city
parlor, or country parlor with a kerosene lamp in it, will
glow with delight over the prospect opened by Harper's
omnipresent magazine. To control by a few touches on a
telegraph at Washington, a river wont to drown vast plantations and engulf cities, is a very pleasing idea. To put four
feet of water, or even "mark twain" on a sand bar is a welcome thought to one who has had to wait the slow action of
crutches on the beef sloughs. But the modest engineers do
not put their "reputations in bond" for any such help below
Lake Pepin. They seem to realize that a river which drains
the watershed of some 3,000,000 square miles can not be
much controlled by a system of reservoirs which commands
the watershed of 5,000, or perhaps 10,000 at most, and that
where the rainfall is not remarkably large. It will be well
for us to build on high ground and expand our ideas of the

size of nature, before we think to get the better of the Father of Waters, and his brood of big sons.

The worst effect of the Mississippi dams on the forests will probably be the indirect one, that in their failure to realize all, or a large amount, of what is expected from them, Congress will be disinclined to spend any more money to defend the river from the loss of its trees. That matter will be left to the States. The States will rely on laws restricting lumbermen and settlers. But the States own little of the land on the headwaters, and law does not execute itself, be it ever so good. The great wilderness embraced by the Mississippi and the Crow Wing will become private property, and its forests will speedily share the fate of all other forests that have existed in this valley—having no mountains or rocks to defend them.

The opportunity to send down to future generations a vast forest standing on level or gently rolling ground, interspersed with charming lakes, navigable rice fields, soft green meadows, and here and there neat villages of intelligent people to whom the lives of trees, from seed to maturity, are almost as sacred as those of animals, will be lost if not seized soon. Think of travelling through such a country by alternate steamer and coach, where even now it is somewhat delightful to do it by bark canoe, while between the lakes one Indian carries the boat and another the paddles and your baggage, while you travel the narrow trail, sometimes wading a little through meadows and tamarac swamps. And all this while this country is yielding more valuable timber than ever it did before, besides better performing the great vital function of purifying the atmosphere for the benefit of all living beings.

Premising that the Chairman of this Committee has for the last ten years been pretty well acquainted with the country about the group of lakes which will be made one if the twelve-feet dam at the outlet of Gull Lake should be constructed, we will say that he has recently visited the sites of the three constructed dams, and with all the better opportunity for observation, in that he failed of enjoying the facilities of travel in government steamer, courteously accorded to him by Major Allen, the superintending engineer at St. Paul. He was fortunately accompanied by Mr. William P. Jewett, a worthy son of the late Charles Jewett, the well-known temperance lecturer, a surveyor, and author of the sectional map of Minnesota, appointed by Governor Hubbard to look into the subject of this report in the interest of the State, which is proprietor of much land concerned.

We started from Brainerd, Minnesota, on Saturday, August 16, at 1.30 P.M., with a good two-horse team and an excellent driver, in the direction of Red Sand Lake. By missing our way, however, we came to a different lake, where a new settler had put up a comfortable house. It began to rain powerfully, but trusting to rubber covering, we did not stop. Retracing our steps, we found the right road, which led us by the beautiful Red Sand Lake without an outlet, and into the old Chippewa Agency road from Crow Wing to Leech Lake. It threads its tortuous way between Gull, Long and Round Lakes, to a log bridge across Pine River, which below the bridge, expands into almost countless lakes. Here a solitary settler, Bartley, has established a homestead, with extensive corn fields and numerous barns. The distance from Brainerd is over 30 miles. Delayed as we were by loss of our way, and driving under a rainy sky, we did not reach Bartley's till 10.30 P.M. It was utterly dark and he and every soul with him were asleep. They arose cheerfully and soon set before us a hot supper. We were specially cheerful because our horses' feet had not slipped through that log bridge. The next day was fine and our road to Leech Lake had on it two human habitations, capable of entertaining strangers, one at 24-mile creek, kept by a half Indian family, and one at 14-mile creek, kept by a family from Maine, in a very commodious log house with out-buildings. Here we dined as well as we could have done at any civilized hotel. The landlady, with only a female domestic and a child of her own race, and whose husband was seldom at home, had not seen the face of a white woman, she said, in six months. We did not blame her for expressing decided discontent.

Arriving at the Leech Lake Agency at 6 P.M., we were half an hour too late to avail ourselves of a pass on the Government steamer. It was fortunate for our opportunity of observation. We saw how white pines were growing upon that neck of land. We hired a bark canoe and three Indians, William Bungo, Basset, the hotel keeper, and Hanks, a vigorous and full-blooded typical Indian, for a voyage, at two dollars a day, as long and as far as might be necessary, including time for their return, and laid in the necessary stores of pork, beef, crackers, coffee, canned fruit, &c., &c. At 11.30, August 18th, we embarked and proceeded prosperously, dancing over the light waves to Otter Tail Point, an elevated promontory overlooking the green and low-lying shores and islands of a most picturesque lake. The indentations forbid that you should ever be out of sight of land. A finer site for a superb summer hotel than Otter Tail Point is not to be found. We dined there on what our Indians cooked. Then they pulled us across three foot waves to the outlet, which ran through, in numerous channels, forests of reeds worthy of the Nile, looking like an immense field of corn sown broadcast, with here and there a cut-off not wider than the canoe. Arriving in good season we were most hospitably entertained by Mr. Blankinghorn, the officer in charge of the dam. The width of the valley makes it a very extensive work, both as to the wooden structure and the embankment, and it is intended to raise the water eight feet.

The next day we threaded our way back through the reed-embowered channel, and proceeded up the northern spur of Leech Lake, the extreme end of which is a navigable rice field. It is like sailing through a field of rye, as high and two or three times as thick as any that ever grew in Massachusetts. It is not always so thick, but often very sparse. When it is ripe, in September, an Indian — probably a female — in a canoe, armed with two sticks, with one bends the grain over the boat and with the other beats it off. Another Indian propels with a paddle. The process is wasteful, but soon fills the boat. To hull it requires thorough drying, after which it is said to be often buried in bark-lined holes, so that the Indian is perhaps the inventor of the silo.

The wild rice, or *Zizania aquatica*, is no near relative of our Carolina white rice, but in flavor and nutritiveness far superior. While in its florescence, it looks like rye and oats growing on the same stem, the oats below the rye. Endowed with such amazing vitality and fruitfulness, the wonder is that it has not been adopted into civilized society and is not flourishing in hundreds of ponds in New York and New England.

Here we made our first portage to a small lake between Leech and Winnibigoshish, pronounced Winnibigo-shish by the Indians, and Winnibi-goshish by some of the engineers. To explain what a portage is, it is necessary to say that our Indians when they entered the service, were clothed like gentlemen down to trousers, stockings and good boots. But they took off both the latter and rolled up the trousers. When they came near the portage and the bark boat was aground in shallow water, they stepped out, took us pooseback and carried us to dry land. Then they dragged the canoe on to it. Then they made up its contents into two packs for two of themselves. The other took the boat on his head, bottom up, as if it were an old Continental officer's chapeau, and trotted off to the next lake with it. The trail of the portage is generally pretty deep, and in low places in wet weather is practically a small canal, perceptibly too narrow for a man who turns out his toes much in walking. When we reached Winnibigoshish by two portages, during which we had excellent opportunity to admire some parts of the native forests, and to deplore the desolation of other parts, a rain storm came on, and we enjoyed the convenience of using the bark canoe as a roof to protect us from it. The rain ceasing, we embarked and our Indians pulled us down the lake to its northern extremity, where the Mississippi rolls out of it in a south-easterly direction. We reached the dam after dark, and were generously entertained by Mr. Harrison, the engineer in charge. As we could see nothing on our arrival we used the next day to look about. The morning was too rainy to proceed. In fact we were told that the rain gauge indicated a fall of $2\frac{3}{4}$ inches in 24 hours, and might have done a little more only it *ran over*.

We might have started before the day was over, but unfortunately one of our Indians, to-wit, Hanks, had found wherewith to get ferociously drunk, and his comrades had to tie him hand and foot till he became sober, which he surely was the next morning. We started early, the thermometer standing at 43 degrees. Went through little Winnibigoshish, made a portage to Ball Club Lake, in which our Indians traversed an unnecessary mile or two by mistaking the trail. Thence into the river, then out of it at White Oak Point, where we saw some most excellent farming land and large quantities of native hay. Thence through a rice lake, and by another most execrable portage over hills and through worse and worse swamps into the river again. We had better kept the river though six miles longer. Through cut-offs traversing rice lakes we reached the Pokegama dam at 9 o'clock, and hearing that the only steamer on the river was four miles below at the foot of the Grand Rapids, we hastened down to the head of the rapids in a canoe, and thence to the steamer on foot, which we reached at 12 o'clock. This haste was because it was to start at day-light, and was not to be up again for a week. This steamer is a comfortable stern-wheeler, as long as the river is wide, which is about 120 feet. The voyage to Aitkin is about 160 miles, though the distance is but 60. The forests along the shore are hardly broken anywhere, and are luxuriant and beautiful beyond description.

We should have accomplished the voyage in a day and a half under the admirable pilotage of a half-breed Indian, but we encountered, caught in a short bend, a jam, or conglomeration of saw-logs of all sizes and lengths, railroad ties, telegraph poles, etc., well matted together. It took two hours of waiting and working with pike poles before the boat dared to attack the jam in force. When it did, the logs, as far as the eye could reach, began to move down stream, and our steamer reached home through them. The owners of that lumber plainly owe something to the owners of the boat. But possibly they are identical.

Perhaps the details of this trip had better have been omitted, but the Committee has thought it only honest to state what opportunity they have enjoyed to form what opinion they have expressed in this report.

ELIZUR WRIGHT,
GEORGE L. BECKER,
J. B. GRINNELL,
Committee.

www.ingramcontent.com/pod-product-compliance
Lightning Source LLC
Chambersburg PA
CBHW031813220426
43662CB00007B/630